MATTERS OF THE HEART

DIXON, BRIDGET J.

From the heart
BD

Contents

Preface	ix
Author to Author Review	1
Introduction	3
Matters of the heart… what's it all about?	4
The heart is already involved…	6
Purposed to know…	10
God's desired relationship with the heart…	20
Quick recap…	22
Pray, pray, pray …	24
Leave the light on …	30
Aligning the heart and destroying strongholds	32
The condition of man's heart…	47
Who or what are you fighting?	51
So, you have the book …	61
Embrace and invest…	70
Real truth, real change …	77
Don't forfeit …	100
Walking in the newness of life…	106
Ask the Father to help you …	109
Standing on the Word …	112
You are invited…	124

CRYOUT

"Confess"	131
"Repent"	137
"Yield"	142
"Obey"	145
"Uncover"	147

"Triumph"	150
"Be excited about it"	153
In conclusion…	155
About the Author	157

Matters of the Heart self-published by Bridget J. Dixon

No part of this publication may be reproduced, stored in a retrieval system or transmitted in any way by any means, electronic, mechanical, photocopy, recording, or otherwise, without the prior permission of the author except as provided by USA copyright law.

Cover image by Morris L Dixon.

Cover design by Akira. Akira can be reached at akira007@fiverr.com.

Book formatted by Steve Bremner. Visit his website at www.stevebremner.com or email him at fireonyourhead@stevebremner.com.

Book edited by Wordswork Consulting. Email Wordswork Consulting at Wordsworkconsulting@gmail.com for your editing services.

Copyright © 2006 by Bridget Dixon. All rights reserved. Printed in the United States of America.

All scripture is taken from the King James Version (KJV) unless otherwise indicated. Public Domain.

Paperback ISBN: 978-1-7360333-0-2

E-book ISBN: 978-1-7360333-1-9

First Edition: November, 2020

*To God the Father, God the Son, God the Holy Spirit be all Glory,
Honor and Praise, both now and forevermore!*

To my family

To all of the people of God

*To him that hath an ear to hear what the Spirit is saying
(Revelations 2:29)*

God bless you all

Preface

Matters of the Heart is my first book. I'd never considered myself an author, however, this book was written and published because the Holy Spirit inspired me to share my story. It's my prayer that each reader of this book will gain enlightenment of the importance of the relationship between the heart and the truth.

Matters of the Heart includes both, scriptural references and personal insight. God's Word is shared to reflect God's thought on a matter and, personal experiences are inserted to provide glimpses of my personal transition from different places of bondage to new places of breakthrough.

I've fearlessly harkened to the Holy Spirit's leading to share God's Word and, I've included the content He's compelled me to share. God's Word is infallible and stand on its own merit and, I stand in agreement with it. All eyes are pointed to the truth, God's truth, therefore; God's Word is highlighted throughout the book for you to clearly differentiate my thoughts and experiences from His unfailing truth.

I've remained transparent when sharing personal views and here's my disclaimer before I go further. I'm not a doctor in any shape, form or fashion. I don't serve in any facet of the mental health profession. I don't hold a degree in psychology, and I'm not speaking as a subject matter expert. However, I'm accurate in my conclusion about this: The heart has so many layers to it that it must be uncovered and, because there are so many layers, it can cover up so many things. The heart is full of so many unknowns, even to you, its carrier.

Matters of the Heart has much heart! You'll thrive to activate positive change in your life as you seek to uncover the matters of your own heart!

Author to Author Review

One of the toughest things in life is realizing that the world is not always centered on us and we must take steps to be better people. For Christians, this means following God and seeking His heart. The author does an excellent job of expressing the matters of the heart, which is to become better people; not just better Christians. The book is informative, precise, and easy to follow along as well as enjoyable! If you are someone yearning and experiencing a strong desire to gain a greater awareness of seeking God with your whole heart, this is the book for you.

I highly recommend reading this book, as for many will find they can relate to the author's journey of heart. Even those who are just starting their journey and those getting revelation, will find this book fitting as they begin to get in sync with God's will. This book may be the missing link to help you with understanding how important the "inward man, the heart of man" is to God. I often thought while reading "How timely is this book for such a time as now!

The author's delivery gives a unique flare that keeps your interest and gives you what I like to call "food for thought". The writing approach gives you a sense of her sitting across from you sharing her story. So much life illuminates while reading the book that you cannot help but ask God to search your heart, know your heart, and reveal any hidden issues needing deliverance; (Ps 139:23). I refer to this comment as having "spiritual open-heart surgery," waiting on God's diagnosis, and making a choice to pursue a "heart change"!

Arnester White, Inspirational Public Speaker, Author of "A Call to Intercession: Praying for Others: The Time is Now"

Introduction

Do I know you? Have we met before?

Yes, you're that awesome person of greatness that God has been longing to bring forth into an even brighter light! Seek God with all your heart and be enlightened by His truth.

Celebrate as God's paths to abundant life are revealed to you! Choose to walk in the truth that makes you free **(John 8:32)** and, by doing so, you'll gain the benefit of that truth, which is liberation from the strongholds that are rooted by untruths.

Living life more abundantly is the original plan meant for you as indicated in **John 10:10** which states *"The thief cometh not, but for to steal, and to kill, and to destroy: I am come that they might have life, and that they might have it more abundantly."*

Matters of the heart... what's it all about?

The heart of who you are or ever hope to be is already beating on the inside you; however, it must remain pliable to retain its ability to adapt and/or to be purged.

Your heart is the holding cell of your greatest successes and your most agonizing defeats. The matters of your heart are priceless jewels rendering an abundance of information to you each and every day. It's always speaking, always revealing.

You can discover your heart's truths and gain enlightenment to see the specks of what God already fully sees and fully knows about you by listening, looking and considering the proofs of your heart's content.

Maybe, you've heard the phrase, "God knows my heart". The truth is, yes, He definitely does, and He's prepared to reveal it to you.

Let me start this journey by sharing with you how this book came in fruition. I never considered myself a writer. I never thought I'd be a writer or someone who would publish material. The skeleton of this writing started in 2006, April 2006, to be precise. I was inspired to start writing about the heart, so I did.

As inspired, I wrote the framework. I had it copy written and then literally laid it on the shelf. This is true. You can see for yourself by confirming the 2006 copyright date and title in the Library of Congress records. The first framework of this book laid dormant on my closet shelf until …well, until I was strongly inspired by the Spirit of God in July 2020 to retrieve it, review it, revise it and deliver it as an added resource for those seeking true transformation, because true transformation is only derived by way of the heart.

The writing was preserved although I started years ago; it was preserved and, I believe it's being released in its due season specifically for such a time as this! If there was ever a time to remember that God is looking at the heart, it's now.

All that you are, all that you ever hope to be, all that you desire in wanting to help others or in serving in any facet of ministry will come to fruition but only to the measure of the condition of your heart.

Any godly and/or sustainable progress you desire will call for an inward look and acknowledgement of the matters of your heart. Dealing with the matters of your heart is the root of all true and maintainable deliverances.

The heart is already involved...

Whatever is going on with you, your heart is already involved. Whatever it is that you may feel or discern is happening for or against you already involves your heart. This is true. Your heart is the source of what is producing the outcome of the life you presently live whether or not you detect, acknowledged or believed it.

Your heart is where everything resides and the treasure chest from which everything is poured. **Luke 12:34** say, *"For where your treasure is, there will your heart be also."* Your heart is a repository of all of the things that can potentially emerge from you. It is the place where good or evil can reside and the place of which the unspoken words are awaiting opportunity to voice. **Luke 6:45** states *"A good man out of the good treasure of his heart bringeth forth that which is good; and an evil man out of an evil treasure bringeth forth that which is evil; for of the abundance of the heart his mouth speaketh."*

The heart is influenced by many things. In fact, if you or if anyone you know who is living a deceitful life, a life of wickedness, lies, murdering, adultery, fornication, thefts and so forth, understand this – such a lifestyle is a direct or indirect result of your heart's condition if it's yours; or their heart's condition if it's them. To put it plainly; such a lifestyle exists as a result of not acknowledging God, not being thankful to God or not glorifying God.

It's a heart-condition that causes the heart to wander down certain paths, to stay the course or to veer into other lanes. The heart accepts and receives constantly, but it's also the source that pumps out everything that's in it. Everything feeds the heart and the heart eats to its fullness; therefore, the heart must be examined. Everything that it takes in must be sorted out regularly.

A heart that's not steadily infused with God's Word and made to yield to truth is a heart that's still filled with "something". The question is, what is the "something" that it's full of if not the truth? If it's not filled solely with goodness or with pure things, the only remaining possibilities would be that the heart is filled with either a mixture of good and bad things, or at worst; it's filled with all bad things. Of the latter, fear not, there's an old saying that gives us all a glimpse of hope. It states, "There is some good in the worst of us and there is some bad in the best of us."

Nonetheless, the evidence of the heart's content, whether good or evil, will flow out subtly or boldly in its carrier's actions and deeds. The book of **Matthew 15:19** states, *"For out of the heart* *proceed evil thoughts, murders, adulteries, fornications, thefts, false witness, blasphemies:".*

The statement made earlier said that perhaps you or someone you know could be living a life of wickedness, evil and/or deceit. That was a candid statement, I know, and it may have caught you off guard to read such a statement right off. I understand that such a statement can seem judgmental and harsh. It could have easily been misinterpreted as condescending, especially, coming out of nowhere and without a prior explanation.

So, let me pause to explain. The referenced scripture of **Matthew 15:19** points to the heart as being the subdivision where all of the things inside of you live. You see, all of the actions you perform are produced by your heart. I did not generate this thought; I am just the messenger and cannot take credit for it. In **John 7:16**, *"Jesus answered them, and said, My doctrine is not mine, but his that sent me."* That's how I feel in writing this book. I'm only the messenger.

In John 7:16, Jesus explained that the words He had spoken were from the Father. Now, I do not claim to be Jesus, no, not at all, but this book will yield to God's Word. There is no need to wonder whether something is good, bad, true, false, right or wrong when there is a word of God that can settle it. **Romans 15:4**, states, *"For whatsoever things were written aforetime were written for our learning, that we through patience and comfort of the scriptures might have hope."*

All of this is being said to reiterate that the very notion of a life of deception, falsehood, blasphemies, adultery and so forth is possible when the heart is under these influences. Since this thought came from the Bible and not from me, that makes it more than a mere thought; it makes it the truth, God's truth.

Purposed to know...

I know now, more than I knew then when I placed the framework of this book on the shelf, that the Holy Spirit inspired me to write it. The same Holy Spirit urged me to finish it. I thank God for second chances. I cannot tell you how many oppositions were at work trying to hinder the completion of this assignment; but I can tell you that there were many. Thank God all of the oppositions failed.

This book is purposed with concentrated doses of truths, truths that will serve as transporters to bring you into whatever ordained places of liberties that God has for you if you choose to allow it. Even the revelations of your own truths, as they are made known to you from the inside out, will generate new levels of insight and discernment within you.

The book is meant to help shine light in places that are concealed, guarded and limited in vision or to make you aware of the blind spots. Blind spots? Yes. You have them, I have them, we all have them; and we don't know what they are because we're blind to them and, in some cases, blinded by them. However, just because you're unable to see truth does not make what you are blind to unreal. Blind spots hide things that are there even though they're not apparent to you. They're not in your current path of sight. These are things that haven't been exposed to your attention, which is why they're called blind spots. They can be right next to you, slightly behind you, so to you, yet, you simply cannot see them. Again, we all have blinds spots.

It takes unfiltered truth to bring forth the enlightenment needed to destroy the strongholds of darkness that create these blind spots. Wait a minute - strongholds? Darkness? What are you saying here and where are you headed with this? I referred to strongholds and darkness, but do not be alarmed at these terms. Just think of a stronghold as a thought, an ideology or a belief that's deeply rooted. As a matter of fact, imagine that it's deeply and strongly rooted.

It's so deeply and strongly rooted that it now has a strong voice within you, perhaps because it has been there for years or because it has latched on to something else that's been there for years. Strongholds become so strong that they serve as guards to hold you securely in a certain place based upon your ideology, mindset or heart's condition. Strongholds aren't easily overtaken, but I'm a witness that they can be uprooted and cast down by the word of truth. I believe that's because truth is both stronger and needed in the process of being freed from a stronghold's grip. Bringing down strongholds requires something mightier than the stronghold itself. From my experience, that "something" has always been God's truth. **John 8:32** states, *"And ye shall know the truth, and the truth shall make you free."*

Darkness, as daunting as the word itself sounds, isn't limited to the deep terrible evils that most of us think of when the term darkness is mentioned. I'm not speaking specifically of witchcraft, soothsaying, divinations or some other evil working force. These are all works of darkness, yet you can be in darkness and not be a partaker of any of these practices. Sorry to disappoint anyone, but the darkness that I'm speaking here isn't that deep. Truth is that darkness exists anywhere there is no light, any place there is a lack of knowledge… or for lack of a milder word, where ignorance exits. Darkness can be present wherever ignorance exists, meaning that what you don't know can leave you in the dark. Darkness remains until light is introduced to drive it out. Light drives out darkness, which is what makes enlightenment so powerful. Light can drive out darkness because light is stronger than darkness. **John 1:5** states, *"And the light shineth in darkness, and the darkness comprehended it not."*

A lack of light or ignorance of the truth is what grants darkness its benefit of hiding and abiding. This is what empowers the things hiding within the darkness to remain hidden. That's what makes truth so powerful and why it should be preferred, though truth sometimes manifests with pain or uncomfortable emotions.

The darkness permits hidden things to stay hidden; therefore, it allows things to go unaddressed. They can go undetected as long as they're hidden and unaddressed. They can grow undisturbed as long as they're undetected; thus, they can develop strong roots as long as they continue to grow undisturbed and then become so strong that they transform into strongholds.

These strongholds become like anchors and forts: They settle in to protect. These strongholds, which resulted from little or no enlightenment of ever existing, are in the blind spots. They can be in the blind spot(s) forever. How can you address an issue if you are unaware that it exists? Enlightenment about the blind spot is required to address it. There are innumerable ways enlightenment can happen, but no matter how it happens the darkness is force to recede as the truth is made known.

Psalms 119:130 states, *"The entrance of thy words giveth light; it giveth understanding unto the simple."* A psalmist wrote these words to describe how God's Word served as a light given by God, a light that gave him understanding and understanding to those who embraced it. The psalmist likened God's Word to a lamp and a light to his path in the same **Psalms 119, verse 105**, stating, *"Thy word is a lamp unto my feet, and a light unto my path."*

If God's Word is light, and it is, then there is no light in the absence of God's Word. Pause and think about that for a moment.

Imagine a path without a light. It can become very dark at times, which is why the psalmist was so thankful to have it. God's word was the light, His guidance. It brought illumination in his obscure places. Life without God's Word would be a life where darkness reigns, and it would do so on a major scale.

Something is hidden where there is darkness. I can't say it enough: Whatever's hiding in the darkness will remain hidden until light exposes it.

I believe that God's Word is the light that exposes darkness. His truth enlightens all darkness: It will show you the evil and tell you where it's hiding within your heart. Furthermore, truth not only shines a light: Truth is the light. Truth illuminates so brightly that you're made to see what the darkness has been working so hard to hide.

The Apostle Paul said in **1 Corinthians 13:11**, *"When I was a child, I spake as a child, I understood as a child, I thought as a child: but when I became a man, I put away childish things."*

Paul shares his realization in this scriptural reference that he needed to cease from doing the things that didn't align with his present maturity. Paul was able to put away the things he labeled "childish" because he became enlightened about their negative contribution to his development and growth. The funny thing about Paul is that, for those who may not be familiar with his story in **Acts 9:3**, he came into great understanding about himself and the Lord when he literally encountered a great light. Nothing is hidden in the light. Paul eventually learned through enlightenment that he had to put away some things that he didn't realize he was doing, things that were in his blind spot.

"Hide and Seek" is a game mostly played by children. I hope I can recall the rules correctly. It's been a while since I played the game, but I remember the rules being along these lines:

The game starts when the designator counter turns their head, close their eyes and start to count from home base, which gives the other players time to hide. The goal of the other players is to find a great hiding place that's not easily identified. The counter stops counting after a while to signify that time is up for the hiders to secure their hiding place, announces, "Ready or not, here I come" and begins seeking those who were hidden. The counter's goal (who is now the seeker) is to identify where the others are hiding. When a hider is identified, the seeker calls it out loudly while protecting the home base. The seeker disqualifies the exposed hider from ultimately winning the game by reaching the home base by doing this.

The game of *Hide and Seek* has multiple winners. The seeker wins each time a hider's hiding place is located while keeping them from the home base. The hiders win if their hiding place isn't identified and they make it to the unprotected home base or if they're identified, but somehow still make it to the unprotected home base. This cycle repeats, eliminating the hiders every round until the hider or the seeker ultimately wins the game.

Now, this is how I remember playing the game. My apologies if this isn't the way other people played it or play it nowadays. Like I said, it's been awhile since I have played this game.

Moreover, why am I even talking about this game? I understand that it's just a game that children play, but I think it's a game packed with lessons that can be applied to life. Ok, I might be alone on this thought, but let me highlight a few reasons for using this game as an analogy.

- You can choose to turn your face away from seeing what's trying to hide by choosing not to pay attention to where it's hiding.
- You can keep your eyes closed and refuse to see what's going on. (hint: It's still going on whether you decide to see it or not).
- Time wasted due to hesitating to quickly search out a matter has now given the matter an opportunity to find a great hiding place and possibly make it to the unprotected home base.
- Hidden matters don't want to be identified because exposure may bring an end to their advantage of being hidden.
- Regardless of the fact that there are things that are well hidden, they will come forth in some form or another.
- You can't afford not to search out the hidden matters if you don't want them to conquer your home base.
- Don't leave home base uncovered.
- Sometimes you'll fail at identifying hidden matters.
- Sometimes you'll fail at covering home base.

These are just a few of the many lessons that can be gathered from this child's game.

Home base in this analogy is the inward man: It's the mind, soul, spirit and heart. These are the best hiding places ever, especially, the heart. A heart left unprotected is vulnerable to the things that are entering into it, so protect your heart from the things that will hinder your victory. [1]Victory is defined as a success or superior position achieved against any opponent, opposition, difficulty, etc. You get the victory whenever your heart, which is the home base, is protected by the covering of truth.

One thing man has certainly learned to do is hide. Oh, my! Men are experts at this (by "man", I mean mankind… sorry ladies). Mankind both male and female, are masters at hiding things and hiding themselves. This goes on all the time. Hidden feelings. Hidden agendas. Hidden blemishes. Hidden past. Hidden motives and a million others things. God is always searching man out for truth. God sent a word in **Isaiah 1:11a**, asking, *"To what purpose is the multitude of your sacrifices unto me? Saith the Lord."* It's God who is interested in our when we perform any action, even good actions.

I can't tell you all of the reasons why man naturally leans towards hiding. I think one reason is of "something", perhaps failure, rejection, judgement, punishment or of others knowing who we genuinely are inside. This my opinion, but I drew it from **Genesis 3:10**, when God called for Adam. Adam and his wife were hiding. *"And he (Adam) said, I heard thy voice in the garden, and I was afraid, because I was naked; and I hid myself".* So, Adam, the first man, said that he hid because he was afraid because he was naked.

Fear is not the only reason people conceal truths, but it was Adam's reason. Looking at this more closely, the reason he gave for being afraid was because he was naked. Looking even closer, being naked hadn't made him afraid earlier. The truth is, he was always naked, so what was different now? Truth. Well, another truth made the difference. The truth of their disobedience to God was brought to light. Adam and his wife, who would later be named Eve, now felt the need to cover themselves and hide what was already their reality.

In **Genesis 3:7**, it states, *"And the eyes of them both were opened, and they knew they were naked; and they sewed fig leaves together, and made themselves aprons."*

There we have it, perhaps the beginning of the first game of *"Hide and Seek"*. Their first reaction to hide themselves was generated by fear. Adam said it. He was afraid of his nakedness being seen. While, they covered their outward nakedness, their actions to hide themselves pointed to the reality of something that wasn't hidden. That is, something else was going on that wasn't being admitted by them. There was a hidden thing called disobedience.

They covered themselves with self-made coverings. Man is still using this solution today, the solution of covering up, and truth is still revealing those cover ups. Truth is still revealing the underlining part that's there but isn't being stated, the part that could have been easily overlooked. Yes, the cloaked part that, like Adam, nobody wants to talk about. By Adam's example, humanity has a history of disguising what they don't want seen by others. God has a history of revealing to man that He can even see past what man is willing to show.

God asked Jeremiah this question in **Jeremiah 23:24**, "Can *any hide himself in secret places that I shall not see him? saith the Lord. Do not I fill heaven and earth? Saith the Lord."* This was a rhetorical question. A rhetorical question isn't meant to be answered by the one being asked, because the answer is already obvious. A rhetorical question is only being asked so the one asking it can also answer it, thus, demonstrating their awareness of it and clarifying that they're not ignorant of what should be obvious to all.

There are things that man obviously seeks to hide. There are things that are hidden within man that find its way to that great hiding place of the heart. Thank goodness for the true solution, which is to search it out and inject the truth, which is the serum that will bring everything out of hiding. Truth will identify the real matter at hand and offer your heart the opportunity to protect itself from deception. Truth will prevent the hidden things from ultimately winning at the end, so keep your eyes open, don't put off the search for truth, call it what it is, and don't let any matter overtake your heart with blindness or deception.

---

1. "Victory," dictionary.com, accessed October 31, 2020, https://www.dictionary.com/browse/victory?s=t

God's desired relationship with the heart...

This book wasn't written to be a good read. You may not be enjoying it at all, and that's okay if that's the truth. But having a good read was not the primary motive for the book's inspiration. The purpose of this book is to heighten an awareness of something very important; that's God desires a relationship with the heart, your heart, every man's heart, and the whole heart at that!

God wants you to come to Him whole heartedly, to trust Him whole heartedly, to love Him whole heartedly and to obey Him whole heartedly. Yes, he wants a whole-hearted relationship with you. In every area where your heart may have wandered away, He wants it to fully return back to Him again.

Jeremiah 24:7 states, *"And I will give them an heart to know me, that I am the LORD: and they shall be my people, and I will be their God: for they shall return unto me with their whole heart."* So, there is no distinguishing here of the current status of your belief. God still wants it to be understood regardless of whether or not you're a person of faith who believes.

The connection He desires with every man is through the heart. God takes an interest in every man's heart and is concerned about every matter dwelling within it. It's important that you know this. Keep your heart open to Him. This increased awareness positions you for innumerable victories in life. Oh yes! A heart that's open to God will make you better off and better blessed!

If you should decide to continue reading, remember this vital thing: God is undoubtedly looking at people's heart. Be prepared for liberation If you can receive His truth with an open heart, because that's exactly what you're going to experience. Be ready for emancipation on so many levels. Remember, **John 8:32** says, *"And ye shall know the truth, and the truth shall make you free."*

Quick recap...

Just in case you need more convincing, here are more scriptures that will shine light on some of the things I've shared.

Psalms 119:10-11 states, *"With my whole heart have I sought thee: O let me not wander from thy commandments. Thy word have I hid in mine heart, that I might not sin against thee."*

A deceitful lifestyle exists from living a life out of a heart that has wandered from God's Word or, perhaps, a heart that hasn't yet been introduced to God's Word at all. Such a lifestyle is fed and incubated by the absence of truth, the lack of acknowledgement of God, not enough thankfulness to God and a deficiency in glorifying God.

David makes it known in **Psalms 119:10-11** what was needed for him to keep his heart connected to God. He recognized that he needed to seek God with his whole heart to stay close to God's Word and not wander from it, so he hid the Word in his heart. He hid the Word in a place that he himself couldn't even get away from, his own heart. David stated that he hid the Word in his heart that he might not sin against God. God's Word is that power: It has the unfailing ability to guide the heart away from desires that are contrary to God's will. Notice that David did not seek God half-heartedly. He sought God whole-heartily. He gave his whole heart, good and bad, flaws and all, to seeking God. He never claimed to have power in himself that caused him to remain on the right track. He never asserted that he was a perfect man on his own. You already know if you are familiar with David's story, that he wasn't a perfect man at all; however, he was as a man of prayer and a man after God's own heart.

Pray, pray, pray ...

Pray. Ok, what does prayer have to do with this? Why does prayer have a part in getting to the matters of the heart? You might be asking this question or any of these: What does prayer have to do with anything? Why are we even talking about prayer right now? Why are we shifting attention from being enlightened to focusing on the topic of prayer? I'm shifting to integrate the need to pray because I'm inspired to do so, it's that simple. I told you this whole book was written by the inspiration of the Holy Spirit, and I'm inspired by the Spirit of the Lord to inject the connection of prayer and matters of the heart right here, right now.

To start, prayer is important. Everyone, and I do mean everyone, needs a prayer life. Better yet, everyone needs a healthy prayer life. Why do I believe this? Because prayer is a way of God! There are so many benefits to praying. It's the gateway through which God communicates with you and the way you communicate with God. Prayer is a communion, a conversation held between you and God, the heavenly Father.

No one can force you to do it. You can choose to live a life without prayer, and you may decide to do just that. It's your choice, but let me at least attempt to caution you and perhaps spare you from potential troubles you'll not only encounter but will likely fail to overcome if you choose not to pray. You can't prevent life from happening to you or anyone else. No one can. You can, however, seek guidance on how to handle life's matters as they land on your path. You can seek to be prepared by praying for wisdom, understanding and grace. You'll be better off praying and receiving wisdom from on high, even if that wisdom directs you to an earthly source. It's the best leading as long as it was revealed through seeking God's wisdom. To pray or not to pray? Hmmm, choose as you will, but consider yourself warned.

Seriously, please do not think, not even for a minute, that you'll achieve true deliverance in the absence of talking to God. Your deliverance may be started by some supernatural intervention, but you would have had to have "had a little talk with Jesus" before the process is complete and successful. Seriously, if you don't have a prayer life yet, please start your relationship by talking to God now, today. Do not hesitate to do this or wait until unbearable trouble comes. Why put this off when there are so many benefits to gain through prayer?

You can still live and make decisions without prayer. You can still come up with plans that are seemingly good ones. Your own plan may actually be an excellent plan in and of itself… it just might not be the best plan for you in the particular case you may be facing. Sadly, you'll not know this until that plan, although a good one, falls apart when you need it to work the most. **Proverbs 14:12** teaches us, *"There is a way which seemeth right unto a man, but the end thereof are the ways of death."* I'm just saying, please pray.

Jesus makes this statement in **John 14:6**, *"Jesus saith unto him, I am the way, the truth, and the life: no man cometh unto the Father, but by me."* This verse signifies the need to have a relationship with Jesus as a prerequisite to gaining access to the Father. More so, to begin a relationship with Jesus has the perquisite of the prayer of salvation. You must pray to invite Jesus into your heart. Prayer is so important because prayer is a way of God.

Good self-generated plans fall apart all the time. Thank goodness for the grace of God that's present to help! The grace of God positions you in a posture that allows you to receive help from God. God, the All-Knowing, All-Wise and Almighty "Everything" wants to commune and fellowship with you through prayer. Now, that's a great promise if I ever heard of one! Do not pass up such a grace. Accept the help offered by grace that's available to you through prayer; or otherwise, be prepared to have many dead-end experiences in your life (based upon **Proverbs 14:12**).

I've had a few experiences with dead-ends that may be lending to my reiterating about not trusting your plan over seeking God's plan. Lord knows I'm a witness; I'm a witness, indeed. That's why I can tell you this and prayerfully save you the time of going through it yourself. Plans gathered in the absence of prayer are subject to failure because they were never God's specific plan for you in the first place and, had you prayed, you would have given God the opportunity to make known to you His magnificent plan for whatever it was that you were facing. However, if you choose to figure it out without seeking God, go right ahead, again, it's a personal choice whether to choose to pray.

If it's God's plan you want, then not praying isn't an option. The only way to know God's plan is to ask God. In **Isaiah 55:8-9**, we learn something about God's thoughts and his ways. It states, *"For my thoughts are not your thoughts, neither are your ways my ways, saith the LORD. For as the heavens are higher than the earth, so are my ways higher than your ways, and my thoughts than your thoughts."* These are His words, not mine. This is the reason to seek Him. Seek Him for his thoughts. Seek Him for His ways.

Don't be surprised when seeking Him for His ways that you actually find His ways. In **Matthew 7:7**, we are told *"Ask, and it shall be given you; seek, and ye shall find; knock, and it shall be opened unto you."* Equally so, don't be surprised in seeking Him for His will for your life that you actually find God's will for your life. The whole purpose of seeking God for direction is to gain it and then to actually follow His directions.

God's direction for you isn't the same as your direction for you. As stated earlier, God's ways aren't like your ways nor His thoughts like your thoughts. God's way can't be compared to anyone else's because it's based on His wisdom. God is in a class all by Himself. The wisdom of the smartest man on earth is still foolishness compared to the wisdom that comes from above. In **1 Corinthians 3:19-20** it states, *"For the wisdom of this world is foolishness with God. For it is written, He taketh the wise in their own craftiness. And again, The Lord knoweth the thoughts of the wise, that they are vain."*

Prayer plays a significant part in getting to the matters of the heart. The wisdom revealed through praying will be far better than the wisdom gained in the absence of prayer, because God's wisdom will be the wisdom needed to resolve the core of the real matter. I can guarantee this one thing for sure: The way of God will yield better outcomes for you than the outcomes gained by leaning on your own understanding. It's to your benefit to know His ways. It's to your profit not to seek Him only to carry out your own heart's agenda.

Knowing of God's acts is powerful, but knowing of God's ways is a whole separate and awesome treasure. His ways and His acts are not the same. **Psalms 103:7** says *"He made known his ways unto Moses, his acts unto the children of Israel."* Praying is a "way" of God. Praising Him is a "way" of God. Acknowledging God is a "way'" of God. Being thankful unto God, these are all "ways" of God. God wants His ways to be known and kept by man. God wants our hearts to be subject to His ways.

God's way leads to living an abundant life. Think about it: Life can be lived as He desires, as **John 10:10 states,** … *"more abundantly"*. Which way will you choose: a lifestyle void of seeking God led by a heart engulfed in darkness or a lifestyle of seeking God through prayer, subjecting yourself to His leading by faith by faith in His word? Remember, darkness is simply not knowing or a lack of knowledge.

A heart void of light will remain in deceit. It will be a heart that's not revived, nor repositioned in its best possible state. It will be a heart that's not upright before God due to the lack of prayer and not crying out to God. God, the one who sees the heart and knows it better than anyone else, has been left out of the equation of resolving the matters of your life. Do not let the absence of a prayer life and a choice to self-manage your heart be your reality.

Again, you can't live a full life without God's input. You can't live life whole-heartily without engaging God, the maker of the heart, in the matters of the heart. I know, not everyone will choose to communicate with God, even with me continuously promoting it. There are people who are living their lives to their fullest based on the fullness of their own ability and to the best of their earthly wisdom and knowledge. These people are not all knowing; therefore, some of their ideas, dreams, insights and full potential will go untapped due to not allowing God to reveal what would have made it better and complete had they only prayed.

Pray, pray, pray; because choosing not to pray is to choose to leave your heart in a more partial state than necessary. Life is lived from the heart. Do not live less than whole due to your heart not being fully engaged. Don't live life half-heartedly. Pray, let God help bring you to your fullest in life.

Leave the light on ...

Let's go back a bit to complete points that I was making regarding truth being the light prior to discussing my inspiration to discuss the importance of prayer.

I was leading up to this point and wanted to make sure I shared it, which is that it doesn't benefit anyone to live in darkness when light is available. Please understand that light is definitely available. You were called out of the darkness to live in the light. This is God's plan for you. You were called into revelation, understanding and knowledge granted by God's leading. The proper response that God expected of you was to praise Him for it. Here, the Apostle Peter states in **1 Peter 2:9**, *"But you are a chosen generation, a royal priesthood, an holy nation, a peculiar people; that ye should shew forth the praises of him who hath called you out of darkness into his marvellous light."*

If you have not yet come out of darkness, for whatever reason, then you're still living in it, even now. I know that saying this is another strong implication. However, it's true and is the reality based on how God sees it. Again, I'm not saying these things from a place of haughtiness, pride or condemnation. I'm not being judgmental, condescending or belittling. I'm certainly not being "holier than thou." I yield to remaining transparent in sharing God's bare truth with you as it has been shared with me by His Spirit.

Aligning the heart and destroying strongholds

The purpose for addressing the full matter of your heart is for the destruction of the strongholds that some matters hold. It's not to discourage you by what's revealed but to free you from the negative impacts that are linked to them. Truth goes after the real things that are gripping your heart, holding it captive. Truth be told, the warfare in your life is tied to a heart. The struggles you face are tied to a heart. The enemies you face are tied to a heart. The favor you receive is tied to a heart. The decisions you make and so forth… you get it – are tied to a heart. Everything involves the heart.

Every scenario of life that you can present, all of the actions performed and, all the reactions to those actions are linked to a heart. Whether it's your heart or the heart of another that's connected to yours, it's still the heart's activity that's in operation. Everything flows from it, everything. This may seem farfetched, but it isn't farfetched at all. I see the evidence of it daily.

Yes, in my personal observations, I see the responses and reactions of many people addressing heart-tied situations almost always the same way. I see this day in and day out. Actually, it's very apparent once you start to pay attention to it. Most people are wired to handle the "thing" without ever seeking to understand the heart of the "thing" and without considering that the heart of "everything" is where the "things" stem from.

I confess that for years I was guilty of operating this way. I took the same approach. I dealt with what I thought was the real issue. Now, I know that it was either all I could see or all that I was willing to see at the time. After all, it takes more time to look at the heart than it does to look on the surface and make a judgement call. You can do the latter, but you won't be accurate. God has to show you for it to be accurate. You must take the time to hear what the Spirit is saying and not judge strictly from a place of familiarity and/or outward judgements.

Besides, I learned that what you see in the heart bears on your own heart. When you see truly unmasked hearts and its matters, your reaction to what you see tells you a lot about your own heart. You will react in some form or another. I know this, because you react in some form even when the truth isn't known. The fact that you'll have a reaction will not change. How you react after truth has come, might.

I remember the lesson the Holy Spirit taught me about love. Yes, I learned a personal lesson about love when God was dealing with my heart and revealing the hearts of matters and the hearts of people involved in the matters. I learned that there was a connection between seeing a person's true heart and the revealing of the authenticity of my love. Let me just say that I failed my agape love test. Agape[1] love is a *love so great that it can be given to the unlovable or unappealing. It's love that loves even when it is rejected.* Agape is the charitable[2] love *that loves without changing.*

Agape love is unconditional, unwavering and doesn't shift depending upon the circumstances. I mean, I failed it many times. I'm ashamed to say it, but truthfully, the love I was using to love others failed time after time. This is the naked truth. I honestly admit it. I'm not proud of it. My love failed until I understood what authentic love was and what it was about love that God was trying to teach me. This is when I was able to maintain authentic love.

He taught me to prepare my heart to receive truth by love. Love is the prep work. Yes, love. Put love in all of the places of your being and keep it there. Love must have a place in your mind, soul, spirit, might, strength, speech, actions and, definitely, the heart. Let love be the foundation of all of your foundations. Look in love, listen in love and, walk in love. Let love be the motive of everything. If the motive doesn't tend to true care, rethink it.

Hey, I know that it may be a different message to hear someone say that you must put love in everything, even in your natural work. This isn't a typo. I'm indeed suggesting that you put love in your natural work, in your schooling, in your business, in everything! Love is the prep work you need to have in place if you're ever going to be able to speak or hear the bare truth. Having love in its place will prove to be strength when truth starts to flow.

Believe it or not, everything is not what it appears. Sometimes, truth tugs heavily on the heart, mind and soul and can even impact someone's spirit. I learned that I had to have genuine love, not the lip service love that professes that it's there but genuine, unshifting and unwavering love.

God taught me that the degree of love before seeing the true heart of any matter should not vary after the truth is revealed. The temperature of love should not waver in the least degree toward an individual after seeing their truths. It remains as it is because it's already complete and unconditional. Any wavering of love at all denotes that it was an imperfect love. Wavering love isn't agape love. Agape love is solid, unwavering, never-failing, unconditional and genuine. God doesn't love us more or less; His love for us remains genuine at all times. I'm not saying that God loves everything that we do, but make no mistake about it – He most definitely and absolutely loves us all.

Loving this way can be a challenge until it's perfected. It's possible, but wow, it was a challenge for me at the start of His dealing with me in a different way. He started to reveal hearts. Every time I thought my love was there, revelation of truth would test my love again. I wanted to know truth; however, truth would be so raw that love had to be present. I had to make the choice to leave love in its place and face truth without letting my love be minimized by the truth that was being revealed. I still practice this and dare not stop. Truth can be overwhelming and is even more so without love. Trust me when I say, you will need love to be able to share and bear the truth.

I'm sharing this because, you, too must be prepared when the light of truth comes on. Truth will reveal more than the obvious. Matters of the heart are both small and great and not always easy to embrace. Some revealing comes with hostility, anger, bitterness, pain, sorrow, etc. This is why a prayer life is needed. It's also why, subconsciously, matters of the heart are avoided altogether. It's love that will strengthen you to see truth as a God thing, not a hard thing. This is why the path is often chosen to just not even go "there," which refers to dealing with the real matter at hand. Truth ultimately yields the best reward of freedom. Truth works to produce liberty, and gaining liberty is worth everything that you have to endure to get to the truth of the matters of your heart.

Bearing truth in love isn't the easiest route for the flesh; however, you must bear down and do it if you want to nip things in the bucket. Face the truth about whatever it is, follow God's leading concerning it, keep your heart freed from the clinches of the deception that tried to hide it, be finished with it and move on.

You don't know your full self until you know the truth. If you're not being honest with yourself on matters, you've not yet demonstrated that you can overcome the deception and stay in the realm of love. To acknowledge truth and remain in love is true victory and, to be able to do so is what Christ exemplified towards humanity. Matters of the heart are the real-life truths. Until you're able to see those truths about yourself and others -- good, bad or indifferent -- you don't know yourself. You may have a hope of who you are and how you may handle a matter. But until you're faced with something on more than a hypothetical level, you don't know if what you've told yourself you'll do in a matter is what you'll actually do when faced with it.

Peter proved this to be true. He believed that he would not be offended by Christ and that he would never deny Christ. He was passionate that he would never do such a thing. Christ revealed to Peter that he would, in fact, deny Him and that he would do it several times. Christ was right. Peter denied Him several times on the same night. This account is found in **Matthew 26:33-34** and in **Matthew 33:73-75.**

"Peter answered and said unto him, Though all men shall be offended because of thee, yet will I never be offended.

Jesus said unto him, Verily I say unto thee, That this night, before the cock crow, thou shalt deny me thrice.

And again he denied with an oath, I do not know the man.

And after a while came unto him they that stood by, and said to Peter, Surely thou also art one of them; for thy speech bewrayeth thee.

Then began he to curse and to swear, saying, I know not the man. And immediately the cock crew.

And Peter remembered the word of Jesus, which said unto him, Before the cock crow, thou shalt deny me thrice. And he went out, and wept bitterly. "

You can believe a lie, but it's still a lie. You can tell yourself anything, and others can tell you what they want you to hear or what they want you to believe about themselves. Everyone could be "okay" with it and accept it, even if what's being said isn't the truth. If that's the case, then the agreed collaboration is still based on falsehood. There's still a deception in operation because truth hasn't yet been exposed.

Please, understand this in your spirit. The surfaced issue isn't necessarily the real issue. The real issue comes from within the heart. I was taught this by the grace of God, so I learned to pray, to ask God for insight and to not lean to my own understanding. This aligns with **Proverbs 3:5-6** that says, *"Trust in the LORD with all thine heart; and lean not unto thine own understanding. In all thy ways acknowledge him, and he shall direct thy paths."* This meant I had to take a different approach in seeing, hearing and comprehending that surpassed surfaces. I had to let God look deeper into my heart. I had to allow Him to completely search my heart out. I had to have an open heart to God's will and be willing to let Him deal with me by truth. I had to learn to embrace others in their truths and maintain a genuine love regardless of what these truths were.

It's easier writing about this than it was actually surrendering to doing it. Doing this is humbling, but that's nothing compared to what you gain. The reward is freedom and restoration. It's both regenerating and refreshing to have truth and to watch truth work wonders in releasing you from hidden darkness. There's nothing compared to the joy and peace you experience after a good prayer that brought you face to face with hidden truths or to the progress you gain in your spirit after appropriately dealing with a hard truth and you were able to maintain your love and integrity throughout it. If truth brought you to a place of repentance, that's even better. [3]*Repentance is a change of mind*. Then, by grace, you're made whole. This is so refreshing! So, be humbled, let go of the pride of not wanting to confess your shortcomings. Understand that others also have flaws. Tell the truth about the matter, even if it humbles you to do so. With humility comes grace. **James 4:6** explains, *"But he giveth more grace. Wherefore he saith, God resisteth the proud, but giveth grace unto the humble."*

I thank God for the deliverances I've received so far that have repeatedly opened my eyes. I'm grateful for Him pressing upon my heart to forever strive to stay in tune with His will. I'm glad that I can share with Him all my cares and concerns. He wants to help me with all of the matters of my life. Understanding what I do now, I don't ever want to handle life the way I handled it before. I don't claim to know it all, but I know enough to understand that God's plan is the only plan that will give me God's promised results. I can spend my life dealing with the façade or dealing with the truth.

Oh, I can't tell you the strength and time I spent fighting symptoms – what a waste! What an incredible waste of time. Everyone would be much richer if it was possible to get back pay for all of the time invested in wrong approaches. No, I'm not the only one who has lost valuable time dealing with the fruit and not the root. Dealing with fruit and not the root is a major thing, yet there are many who do it. There's a missed opportunity to get a true victory every time this approach is taken. Sadly, some people are content with just being in the fight and, don't care about winning it. As long as they're working on a matter, true or false, is good enough to some people. This is like fighting the air. Fighting, fighting, fighting "everything" except the "thing" that's opposing them. It's much easier fight to address the fruit of the matter than to fight the root of the matter. The root of the matter is in the heart. The fruit of the matter is the visible part that hangs on the outward branch. Everybody can see it. Truth reveals that there's a deeper problem, but nobody delights in digging to see where the problem is coming from. The matter has a root cause.

The fruit receives the attention most of the time for this cause. The fruit is addressed or even plucked. Rarely is there a pause or a Selah moment to consider that the fruit came from a seed that was planted under the surface long before it came to fruition. It's seldom the first approach to address any matter this way. Apparently, it's just too much of a hassle; besides, addressing the fruit is better than doing nothing. In reality, addressing the fruit only is the root of doing nothing. Addressing the fruit will not yield the real resolve. How can it, when the solution hasn't yet addressed the root of the issue?

Yes, getting rid of fruit is a quick fix. Something to keep in mind is that getting rid of fruit is also a temporary solution. The real matter hasn't been addressed until the heart's contribution to the matter has been addressed. You must get to the heart of the matter. Taking the quick approach yields some quick relief; however, the fruit will reoccur and keep reoccurring until the root cause of its existence is addressed. The recurrence of fruit is absolutely what's likely to happen as long as the root remains. You see this in nature all the time. I pluck plums off my plum tree one year and guess what happens the next year? Plums grow back. The plums come back as long as the tree remains rooted. Without any fertilizing, plums come right back. All it takes is the right season and here come the plums.

Likewise, the return of issues is possible when the real matter feeding the issue, the root cause, isn't dealt with. The issue goes away for a while, but the right season will bring them all back gain. Unfortunately, old rooted and returning fruit is the underlying cause of many things, such as broken relationships, personal failures and barriers not yet conquered. I've heard the stories. I've been asked puzzling questions by someone in their frustration as they were seeking to understand why their relationships continued to fail or how they kept finding themselves repeatedly in undesired or abusive relationships. I've heard the agony and seen the aggravation caused by the rematerializing of old barriers that were left unaddressed.

In talking with people, I've found that most people, like myself, want real breakthroughs and real deliverances that free them from real bondages that temporary breakthroughs can only offer them for a moment. The deliverances God has and wants for you are lasting and truly liberating. It's not God's desire that you repeat and recycle warfare. He wants you to always triumph according to **2 Corinthians 2:14** that says, *"Now thanks be unto God, which always causeth us to triumph in*

Christ, and maketh manifest the savour of his knowledge by us in every place.

Sustainable victory you come as a result of letting God into the depths of your heart. Trusting Him with all of the matters of the heart is how true deliverance is brought into existence. Any victory gained on the fruit level along leaves a stronghold unbroken. The stronghold is present as long as the root remains intact. The breaking of strongholds comes by uprooting the thing that's producing the fruit, which is the budding flower of the bondage occurring beneath. You must be willing to oppose the root cause when it's revealed so you can be free from the stronghold and the bondage. The fruit will remain and will continue to grow back repeatedly without your willingness to do this.

Matthew 12:35 says, *"A good man out of the good treasure of the heart bringeth forth good things: and an evil man out of the evil treasure bringeth forth evil things."* Real change, real results and real solutions aren't solutions that merely rest on resolving problems only on the surface level. A change of heart is needed to experience real change. Oh, I said it, the bare truth. More than a surface change is needed. Something has to change in the core, in the seed of the matter, in the heart.

This truth applies in all situations and in all realms. Even in dealing with the issues of racisms, injustices, inequalities, discriminations and all prejudices of any kind. These prejudices will only be eradicated, like every other evil, by dealing with the root of it. Removing them will require a change of heart. It's never enough to change the outward only. You can change the law to enforce the appearance of equality. Man can perform the appearance of change. The real change happens when it happens in the heart. There's no real change until the heart changes. In other words, if nothing changes in the heart, nothing changes. **Matthew 12:33** says,*" Either make the tree good, and his fruit good; or else make the tree corrupt, and his fruit corrupt: for the tree is known by his fruit."*

The only genuine fruit a tree can produce is the genuineness of its tree-kind. "Tree-kind," yeah, I made that up, but you get the gist. An apple tree can't produce peaches…not real ones. It takes an apple tree to produce real apples. The tree can only produce after its kind. So, either make the tree and its fruit good, or make the tree corrupt and that's the fruit it bears. The change has to occur in the core, the heart.

Since the real issue is coming from something rooted within the heart, the real change must also come from the heart. No exceptions. You must cooperate with the conditions of the deliverance to receive the deliverance. The uncompromised condition in gaining true deliverance is this: The heart must be in the center of the process and fully yielded to whatever God wants to do. Everything about breakthrough and deliverance starts and ends with the heart.

Luke 6:43 teaches, *"For a good tree bringeth not forth corrupt fruit; neither doth a corrupt tree bringeth forth good fruit."* You can end the root cause of corrupt or undesired fruit by refusing to allow your heart to feed on it, or you can be fed by whatever is keeping the undesired fruit nourished. Refuse to be the tree that continues to produce the end results that you don't desire.

Get to the bottom of it. Change your core. Everyone has a heart, and every heart involved in any matter connected to you contributes to the fruit being produced.

You can only choose change for yourself. Be clear on this. Just because other hearts are involved in a matter doesn't mean that you reign over any of the other hearts. You only have power over your own heart. You can only live from one heart, your heart. You can only live from your own heart! Wow! That is a simple but powerful statement. Here's an enlightening revelation: You don't have control over anyone else's heart. Each person can only live from their own individual heart.

People can only treat you well or badly to the measure of the "stuff" housed in their heart. You can only treat others one way or the other based upon the "stuff" in your heart. Ok, I won't refer to it as "stuff" but as content. Everyone's treatment of another is limited to the content of their own heart.

This is another one of the many reasons why it's essential to pray for the heart of every person. Everyone has a heart, and every heart contributes to seeding or feeding the fruit that will eventually manifest if that seed isn't purged from the heart. Keeping the heart purged from things that will hinder godly progress is a perpetual process. It begins with acknowledging that the heart is no good left on its own. Don't mistake the guarding of the heart to mean that the heart should not be allowed to be free. It should be free to learn new things and to be creative but not free to roam wherever it likes without a chaperone. The heart needs guidance and can't guide itself. It should not go unchecked, even for a day. Remember the game of hide and seek: The heart is too risky to trust on its own. It's the home base that needs protecting, not from creativity, innovation or the embracing of new ideas, but from protected filters that won't allow the entrance of light. God's Word and prayer serve as perfect guides. In the midst of receiving godly instruction and praying, God is invited to examine the heart and to show the heart's condition. Through the light of the Word and prayer, your heart and the hearts of others should always be lifted up before God.

Once you're enlightened with truth, take every action needed to eradicate unwanted contributing factors from your heart. **Matthew 3:10** says, *"And now also the axe is laid unto the root of the trees: therefore, every tree which bringeth not forth good fruit is hewn down, and cast into the fire."* Sometimes, a fresh start is needed. No worries. Getting to the root of matters tends to feel like you're starting all over again. This isn't necessarily a bad thing. It's a good thing when you're purged from things that hinder the good fruit from coming forth. Once those conditions are removed, you'll grow stronger and reach new and higher heights.

I have a jewel for you, something valuable to embrace. It's called wisdom. Here's a word of wisdom for you that you should hold on to: Stay in alignment with God by keeping your eyes on the things that matter to God. Learn to agree with Him. Love what He loves and hate what He hates. This is the jewel I was referring to, it's value is priceless and should not be sacrificed for anything.

1. "Agape," Blueletterbible.org, accessed August 26, 2020, https://www.blueletterbible.org/Comm/guzik_david/StudyGuide2017-1Cr/1Cr-13.cfm?a=1075001
2. "charity," Blueletterbible.org, accessed August 26, 2020, https://www.blueletterbible.org/Comm/guzik_david/StudyGuide2017-1Cr/1Cr-13.cfm?a=1075001
3. "Repentance is a change of mind," Blueletterbible.org, accessed August 26, 2020, https://www.blueletterbible.org/lang/lexicon/lexicon.cfm?Strongs=G3341&t=KJV

The condition of man's heart...

Why focus so much on the heart? The condition of the heart matters. The thing that grieved the heart of God as recorded in the Book of Genesis was the condition of man's heart.

Genesis 6:5-6 says, *"And God saw that the wickedness of man was great in the earth, and that every imagination of the thoughts of his heart was only evil continually. And it repented the LORD that he had made man on the earth, and it grieved Him at His heart."*

The condition of the heart is important. It's the reflection of our core. We lead with the heart. Take a look around, listen to yourself and to others. Be the judge for yourself on whether what I'm saying is true or not. Let your eyes see; let your ears hear; better yet, take a moment to consider your own approaches in matters, any matter, especially, those matters that you concluded weren't in your favor. Those cases are the best ones to review when searching out matters of your heart. Since most people do well in responding to matters that are resolved in their favor, let's take a look from a different angle. What about the opposite? How does your heart handle unfavorable outcomes?

Pause now and take a self-assessment. It's just a little examination of the other side of the heart. You must allow the whole heart to be examined when surrendering the whole heart. Your answers are always on the honor system and just for you. Take a minute, think about it and answer truthfully.

Engaging Activity:

Answer the five simple questions below. See if you can track the rhythm of your heart's response when it's faced with matters that aren't so favorable. Think about an experience or an encounter to your heart that wasn't so good. Maybe you were offended or maybe you were the offender. Maybe you were wounded, disappointed, rejected or wronged in some way or another.

- Did you address the matter?
- Did you pray to get God's direction before addressing the matter?
- Did the steps produce a positive and godly outcome?
- How did you treat the person(s) involved?
- Did your love for the person(s) change or shift in any degree?

Maybe you did everything right, maybe not. Why is it necessary to self-examine? The questions aren't meant to accuse you; they're helpful in getting you to pay attention to what flows out of you. You can see the proof of the content of your heart by your actions. Searching your heart continuously can be agitating, because it challenges you to stay connected with the actual demonstration of the behaviors. This is why you were asked to examine a past matter, one where the reaction was already complete. It may seem like just a petty cliché, but hindsight really is 20/20. These real-life examples will help you identify your real heart's condition. It will reveal whether the fruit that flows from your heart is healthy or whether additional work is needed to release the undesired fruit being produced.

I received a course grade and a conduct grade when I was in school. The course grade was the result of knowing the subject at hand. The conduct grade was based on the behaviors I displayed. The conduct grade mattered just as much to my mom as the course grade. Her theory was along the lines of you don't have to be the smartest student to have great conduct. The conduct grade was granted based on the character you exhibited. Conduct, like everything else, is influenced by the heart. Good behavior takes discipline.

This is why it's necessary to probe your heart with penetrating questions. The heart holds an abundance of information. It serves as a locator. Yes, an open and honest heart will tell you exactly where you are on the journey to wherever you're trying to go. Your starting point isn't where you have to stay. The good news is if where you are doesn't reflect where God wants you to be and, you're willing to change, you don't have to stay anchored in an undesirable place.

This journey is all about strengthening your heart. It's all about becoming better, becoming more refined, purged where needed and renewed. Every beating heart certainly has the need to be strengthened. No one's heart, and I do mean no one's, has reached or will ever reach the status of not ever needing a "heart-fixing." There's always something in there that can stand a little work. No one's heart is ever fully exempted from being wrongly influenced, so no one's heart should ever be exempted from being lifted up before God in prayer for help.

Just as love is a preparer and prerequisite for bearing truth, a good heart search is the prerequisite for preparing the heart to address real battles. This is a key that bears repeating. You aren't resolving the real matter if you haven't been brought face to face and heart to heart with the real matter, so be courageous, honest, open and ready to see the real opponent. Don't settle for the surface alone, dig deeper under the surface. Let the truth that comes to you bring with it the deliverance that it's designed to produce. Don't let the devastation of truth destroy you. Get past the devastation of its blow through love and grab hold of the benefit because, there is truly a benefit. Truth gives an advantage against deception. Awareness of things needing to be purged to become stronger, wiser, and victorious are heightened by truth. Yes, truth shows what's hiding in the dark or dwelling in the blind spot. Truth gives insight to handling matters in a way that will bring forth the fruit of awesomeness that's awaiting to spring forth. Oh yes, this whole experience of liberation by way of dealing with the heart's truth is awesome!

Who or what are you fighting?

Getting to the place of awesomeness and to life more abundantly is a process. This will require you to press forward, and fight for it. My, my, my, I never wanted to be a fighter because I love looking on the brighter side. I love remaining hopeful, inspiring others to do the same, being joyful and abiding in peace as much as possible. Truth is, there's no real joy or peace inside when you're facing one opposition after another. Sometimes you have to deal with oppositions to get to the inner joy and peace desired. The opposition will take away your praise, your inspiration, joy, peace and everything else it can take. You'll have to overcome opposition to maintain your real joy and peace.

Yes, you'll have to suit up, armor up and fight. You won't be as prepared for the fight as you could be, without facing the truth. I've said it before, truth can be tough to hear and I can testify to that. I can also testify that you won't overcome without truth. The second and third chapters of the Book of Revelation addressed seven churches and each one had something to overcome. They were told the truth of what they needed to overcome, prior to being told the reward they would gain for overcoming. These churches had to deal with the root cause and true matter that was hindering them from their ultimate victory. They were told what the oppositions were. They were introduced to their true opponents.

A strategic fighter doesn't come out swinging at the air. This method might land a few hits every now and then, but it isn't the best strategy. The plan of a skillful fighter involves the intentional landing of deliberate punches to the real opponent with every punch. That's the strategy of a real fighter because that's the strategy that produces a win.

You need to know the real target so you can hit it. The target tells you where to aim; otherwise, you'll waste time and energy addressing everything else, except the real issue.

Those who seek true liberty don't hide behind aimless swings, forms and fashions. They aren't afraid to face their true opponent. Here's a well-kept secret you may not know: The opponent is never a person. The real opponents are never "people." I know, the opponent's appearance can look like a person and opposition can certainly manifest through a person. Believing that an actual "person" is the root problem is the act of deception at work. **Ephesians 6:12** teaches, *"For we wrestle not against flesh and blood, but against principalities, against powers, against the rulers of the darkness of this world, against spiritual wickedness in high places."*

The real things we wrestle with, fight and contend with aren't people. I can't say it enough, people aren't our real opponents because they aren't the real issue. The real matter is more than what meets the eye. Making you think that people are the sole problem is the greatest trick used by your enemy. It's a ploy to keep you swinging at the air in the dark and missing your target every time. This is another strategy of darkness: Bringing obscurity and blinding the eyes from seeing the real issues is a trick that just keeps working. The enemy uses this tactic because it works! It's an old, ancient trick, but it still works. The real opponent is behind the façade, dwelling underneath the lie and remaining unidentified. It's this deception that's at work with the goal of preventing you from getting to your real victory.

Paul puts it this way in **1 Corinthians 9:26-27**, *"I therefore so run, not as uncertainly; so fight I, not as one that beateth the air: But I keep under my body, and bring it into subjection: lest that by any means, when I have preached to others, I myself should be a castaway."*

Wow! That is a good word! It's a short passage, but it says a lot. Paul is sharing insight of his fighting strategy. Look at all of the approaches Paul took that are mentioned in these two verses:

- Paul understands the path that he's chosen and isn't running in uncertainty
- He understands that he will fight certain battles and, is ready and willing to do it
- Paul has a fighting strategy and prepares himself to fight with purpose

- He refuses to hit and miss by swinging at everything around him
- He aims at his true target, the very thing in opposition, in an effort to finish his race
- Paul is looking for progress and holds himself accountable

It appears that Paul wants a real win. He has a plan to face whatever opponent necessary to cross the finish line. This is a great list of things that should not be ignored when desiring a win. This mindset is another priceless jewel. Paul's focus wasn't on what others around him were doing. He wasn't focused on others. His strategy focused on the things he needed to be prepared for to achieve the best outcome. He likened the lack of preparation to the beating of the air. He purposed to win by certainty, not by hitting and missing or what he refers to swinging at uncertainties.

Paul deliberately prepared to go after the true thing that opposed him. He aimed at overcoming the true obstacle. Paul didn't appear to be concerned about the symptoms the race presented but at gaining the victory at the end. Fighting against the matter's symptoms and not against the real matter is the same as beating at the air. Actions, responses and tactics that only put the fire out on the surface are an incomplete response, because that fire is most likely to blaze up again.

Paul puts it this way in **1 Corinthians 9:26-27**, *"I therefore so run, not as uncertainly; so fight I, not as one that beateth the air: But I keep under my body, and bring it into subjection: lest that by* *any means, when I have preached to others, I myself should be a castaway.*

Wow! That's a good word! I hope you got that. It's a short passage; but it's saying a lot. Paul here shares insight of his fighting strategy. Look at all of the approaches taken by Paul that are mentioned in just these two verses:

- Paul understands the path he chose and is not running in uncertainty
- He understands he will fight certain battles and is ready and willing to do it
- Paul has a fighting strategy and prepares himself to fight with purpose
- He refused to hit and miss by swinging at everything around him
- He aims at his true target; the very thing in opposition to finishing his race
- Paul is looking for progress and holds himself accountable

Paul takes full responsibility for being disciplined enough to come to complete victory. He stated in the second part of the referenced scripture, **1 Corinthians 9:27**, "*But I keep under my body, and bring it into subjection: lest that by any means, when I have preached to others, I myself should be a castaway.*" Paul holds himself accountable and doesn't excuse himself from preparing for the victory. His strategy looks at every part, including the part he plays.

I've seen people go full force at an issue. They go ruthlessly straight after the fruit of the issue without considering for one moment, at the least, that the heart of the matter is the real opponent. They pass right by the real issue and aimlessly beat the air. This approach is taken by some of the wisest, greatest and smartest people I know, people you'd think "just should have known better." However, some of the strongest of the strong have been guilty of handling matters this way.

Honestly, I've been guilty of this myself. My eyes had to be enlightened to stay focused on the heart of the matter, and even on the heart itself. Many times, I jumped in the ring and was going at it, beating at the air. Oh, and I'm not alone in this confession and, if given the chance, you'll probably admit that you've been guilty once or twice of mishandling a situation or two in your life as well. Maybe, given the chance, you'd also admit that you've been guilty of focusing on the fruit of the matter versus the root of the matter.

But – it's a new day! The light has come. We've learned to suit up and fight the right fight. Now that the invisible opponent in the ring is made known and, it's craftiness to remain hidden in the concealed and undisturbed places of the heart is understood, it's time to use this advantage to overcome its stronghold. Living life as an overcomer increases your liberty. Deception's stronghold will lose its ground as truth becomes known. You can move forward rejoicing in the truth that redeemed you and, live free from the hindrance of everything that fought you in and through darkness.

This is now an ongoing goal for me. I pray for my heart and mankind's hearts all the time. I remember when the Holy Spirit first quickened me to do this. It was such a strong anointing like I'd never experienced before. I prayed and prayed. I prayed so many prayers as I was led to do in lifting up the hearts of men before God. My heart was never to be excluded in these prayers. I prayed and I prayed. I prayed in my private prayer time. I prayed in churches. I prayed with groups and individuals. So many prayers were prayed for the hearts of men.

Then, I was led by the Holy Spirit to teach about the heart. Teach about the heart, teach about the heart, teach about the heart. This reiteration isn't a typo. I was repeatedly led to teach about the heart, so, I did, repeatedly. I spent months teaching on the heart and still barely touched the surface. God has a lot to say about the heart! It's inexhaustible. The hardest part about completing this book was knowing that there was so much more about the heart that I would not be able to cover in this single book. This entire book is a small token of my contribution toward highlighting the need of placing attention and importance on the heart and the matters of the heart.

Focusing on the heart is absolutely not in vain. God wants His people to understand the importance of the heart and how much the heart matters to Him. God wants His people to change what they're fighting and, how they're fighting life's battles. He wants them to examine the position of the heart in every matter faced because matters of the heart go deeper than what's realized by most people. Yes, the heart is a place of great depth. There's a lot of "stuff" in there. Okay, okay – content.

There's a lot of content in there. This is why God has so much to say about the heart. This is why He is so vested in bringing the truth to the heart.

I was led to witness about the heart in many places as God was opening the doors of discipleship. Seeing that the heart is the place where all matters reside, God allowed me to use every platform made available to me in ministry to direct man's attention to the heart, even if it was just through a prayer. Every ministry group or audience of faith that I faced at that time God was using it as an opportunity to share the need to the examine the heart. There were so many conversations that I was seemingly thrust into about the heart. It was as if God was supernaturally placing me right there in the conversation and was giving me the opportunity to talk about it. It was an ordained time for sure. God was just opening doors in these different ministry forums to have these discussions, time and time again. Over the phone, in class, in service, at home, in Bible study, in the community, in ministering abroad, to the young and to the elderly – God kept talking about the heart. Yet it seemed to have barely touched the tip of the iceberg in comparison to all that God desired to say about it.

I was doing all I could to speak about the heart but, as you can see, it was a lot to cover. I'd developed a passion for talking about it because it was coming from a place of personal deliverance as well. All of the praying and studying about God's concern for the heart and its matters had an intimate effect on my heart. The understanding of how God wanted to deal with the heart was working as a source of deliverance for me. I knew that this was a revelation from God and He wanted to help all of us in this manner. I knew I had to get people to take a different action than the actions I'd witnessed or performed myself. I urged them to consider this approach. I urged them from a place of obedience to God and, as a sincere witness of the great results I was starting to experience from this revelation.

I urged them to just try it. Try praying about the heart of the matter and the hearts of man before going toe to toe with what seemed to be the issue. Pray for the heart? Yes, pray for the heart! Pray for the hearts of those who are hurting. Pray for the hearts of the people who are bitter and angry. Pray for the hearts of the rejected and those who are mislabeled by society. Pray for the hearts of those who are confused and are being influenced by deception. The prayer list for the heart is endless because whether a person is deemed to be great, small, good or bad by anyone's standard it doesn't remove the fact that everyone has a heart, a heart that needs prayer.

I passionately asked people to take their eyes off the pain they were experiencing because of a particular matter, even if it was just for a moment. I asked them to embrace the mindset from the pain, frustration, whatever it was they were focused on. I asked them to embrace the mindset that ceased from catering to only what they were seeing on the surface or feeling emotionally. I asked them to look past those levels and to be open to see the real issue as revealed by love, truth and the light of God's Word so they could obtain the real solution.

It was difficult for some, however, those who were willing to listen and do that came to realize this truth, that the real matter was never what it appeared to be on the surface. The root cause is never fully revealed outwardly. As the old saying goes, "You can't judge the book by its cover," not even this one because the cover is just that – a cover. The core or the content of a book is hidden within just as the heart of the matter is always abiding within.

So, you have the book ...

As I mentioned earlier, the Holy Spirit quickened me to reach back and retrieve the framework of this book that I'd started years ago. I was suddenly led to finish it. I've obviously finished it now so that you and many others would have it in this season. I'm certain that now is the time that it was ordained to be shared, and now is the time for you to have it and gain a greater awareness of the need to seek God with your whole heart on all the matters of your heart.

Now is the divine time to get this down in your heart or at least to put this message in the hands of someone you know who will benefit from hearing the information this book contains. Now is the time for everyone who doesn't realize it to finally see the truth that resides in their heart. A truth that's there but so deeply hidden that it isn't yet recognized.

The heart of man is God's concern, but not only the heart, its matters and everything it houses. God's concern is for the heart of every man, whether saved, unsaved, rich, poor, young, old and regardless of race, nationality or creed. Every living man, friend or foe, an enemy to you or God, their current status doesn't matter; their heart is a concern to God. It's time to regain or perhaps increase focus on repairing the one thing that will bring a sustainable difference in every man's life, which is a heart turned back and submitted to God and truth.

The urgency to complete this book was so pressing that I immediately took vacation time away from work to answer the call of focusing on its progression. After years of the skeletal framework lying dormant on my shelf, in a matter of moments I was compelled to complete it. The need to complete it was to share that true transformation is possible.

This book wasn't birthed out of convenience. It wasn't brought forth in a season void of hardships. So much was going on in the world during the time I was finishing this book. People everywhere were experiencing new norms. Death tolls were on the rise from an unforeseen virus that was impacting the entire world. The whole world seemed to have been in a shaking, plus, there were other major issues of racism, protests, injustices, inequalities, discriminations, etc. I had many things on my plate, too, with this little thing called a personal life. I took heed to the call of finishing the book during all of this because the Spirit said, "Now" – and that settled it. It was now time to finish it.

Writing the book is an act of obedience. The sharing of my personal experiences is in no way an indication that I'm the subject matter expert on heart matters. The completion of this book isn't an insinuation that I'm a finished work or that I have "arrived" to all of my glorious victories. The truth is just the opposite. I have not arrived. I go through this process repeatedly, gaining new victories each time. I've made progress, but I've not totally arrived and neither have you. No offence, just another dose of truth.

1Corinthians 10:12 says, *"Wherefore let him that thinketh he standeth take heed lest he fall."* It would be unwise and dangerous for anyone to think that no further.

So, why listen to me? Why take the time to read my story, hear my testimonies or consider what I'm saying if I'm not the acclaimed expert on matters of the heart? Why listen to me if I'm still a work in progress? The answer is simple: For whatever reason, God started revealing to me very strongly that the matters of the heart matter to Him. This added benefit to my life. I hope you'll allow Him to speak with you concerning your heart. I want you to receive the benefits he has for you concerning your own heart. Take the time to hear what the Spirit of the Lord is saying to you.

Count my story valuable or not. It's valuable to me. I was loved by God with all my flaws, and there are many, yet He took interest in the matters of my heart. He loved me into a better place. He cared for me. He still cares for me. I'm fully persuaded that He cares for the heart of every man. The best part about His caring is His ability to do whatever is needed to overthrow the things that attempt to minimize freedom. He will take you to your high place in some miraculous way.

Habakkuk, a prophet in the Old Testament, came to this conclusion. **Habakkuk 3:17-19** reads,

"Although the fig tree shall not blossom, neither shall fruit be in the veins; the labour of the olives shall fail, and the fields shall yield no meat; the flock shall be cut off from the fold, and there shall be no herd in the stalls; Yet will I rejoice in the Lord, I will joy in the God of my salvation. The Lord God is my strength, and he will make my feet like hinds' feet, and he will make me to walk upon mine high places. To the chief singer on my stringed instruments."

Habakkuk settled with the truth that God will come through for him despite the challenges he faced. He made the choice to rejoice in the God of his salvation. I choose joy. The weeping may come, but joy empowers me to press forward.

God's Word will show you that what I'm sharing with you is true. The scriptures show us that God addresses the core of matters. He doesn't shy away from the real issue at hand, so why should we? He looks at the heart of man, the central location to which everything is tied. Speech involves the heart, and actions result from matters of the heart. Even the transformation of salvation involves the heart. God's Word, meditating on that Word and becoming a doer of the Word will strengthen and correct the heart as it embraces God's truth and follow God's leading.

This book is a release of my personal account of what God, by His Spirit, helped me to see about my own heart. I'm sharing how I started receiving better outcomes in life just by focusing on the things that He directed me to focus on. I'm nowhere near a finished work. I can probably find about a hundred witnesses that will testify to that at any given time. I'm not finished, because God's not finished with me. God will be working on my heart as long as I have breath in my body.

Philippians 1:6 says, *"Being confident of this very thing, that he which hath begun a good work in you will perform it until the day of Jesus Christ."* It's an ongoing process. It's also an ongoing benefit to keep trusting and allowing Him to do a work in me. So, I've made a personal decision to let Him do whatever He wants to do in bringing my heart upright. I count that an honor and happily submit to it.

I've learned to trust God with my whole heart and with the hearts of all men. For me, this is very liberating! It changed my way of praying and it changed my life. Whenever I find myself struggling with a matter, He reminds me to bring the full matter before Him. I empty out my heart to Him and then I wait. I listen. I keep my ears open to His leading by His word, and I make the commitment to follow His leading. I choose to yield to His way. I now love to yield my heart to truth, and I love the renewal, redemption and restoration that results from doing so. It's my everlasting prayer for every man's heart to be lifted up before God. Besides the prayer of salvation, praying that the hearts of others are in the hands of God is the best prayer that I can pray for them. Even the prayer of salvation deals with the heart. No one except God can accurately discern the motives and intent of every man's heart. The best I can do is turn it over to Him.

This book helps to expose the hidden strategies of the true adversary. It was time to reveal these manipulative operations of the enemy. He seeks to offset the greatest outcomes of your life by keeping the real matters unexplored. Whatever part I was blessed to understand about this, however small, it was time to share it with as many people as possible. It was time to contribute whatever small piece I could to help anyone I could to become free. It was God's timing.

Mordecai told Esther concerning moving in God's timing and for God's purpose these words found in **Esther 4:14**, *"For if thou altogether holdest thy peace at this time, then shall there enlargement and deliverance arise to the Jews from another place; but thou and thy father's house shall be destroyed: and who knoweth whether thou art come to the kingdom for such a time as this?"*.

Just as it was time for Esther to speak out at that time, I believe it was time for me to speak out now. This is the time to heighten awareness concerning your heart. For some, it's a season for seeding; for others, a season of harvesting. The good news is that God supplies everyone with what they need in every season. Pray. Ask God to show you the true purpose of you obtaining this book in this season. Make it more than a read. Make it a personal journey. Start here.

Here is another interactive opportunity, a prayer. Start with the model below and add to it as you're led to do so. The main thing is that you pray. Pray for insight and revelation from God about matters of your heart.

Heavenly Father, again I come seeking you.

I seek you for direction *and insight.*

According to **Psalms 119:105**, *"Thy word is a lamp unto my feet and a light unto my path".*

Let your truth reign in my heart.

Free me from every work of darkness hiding in my heart.

My heart is open to hear your voice and to understand what you are speaking to me in this season.

Whatever reason you allowed this book to land in my hands, let me receive your will; nothing more, nothing less.

In thou Son Jesus' name I pray. Amen.

The goal of this book is simple: It's to bring you to a sobering truth, the truth that it isn't only possible but highly probable that many are living half-hearted lives. By half-hearted, I mean never accomplishing their personal aspirations or God-given visons because the full heart is either not engaged or not fully engaged. A heart half-engaged in the vision can only produce a result that's half as successful as it was intended to be.

God, the All-Seeing God, must be allowed to continually guide you through matters of your heart and the sorting out of the content of your heart to keep it in the best condition. This sounds great; however, it isn't always easy to keep your heart upright. To keep your heart aligned with God's will for you will require the pain of pricking.

Acts 2:37 states, *"Now when they heard this, they were pricked in their heart, and said unto Peter and to the rest of the apostles, Men and brethren, what shall we do?".* Pricking is painful, but if the message of truth that pricked the heart is embraced, pricking works for the good. Being opened to truth is vital and good for the heart. Being opened to truth is also needful for transformation. Filters that block truth can also stop you from taking the actions necessary to experience the full manifestation of what that truth was intended to release you from and release you into.

As with the case just referenced in **Acts 2:37**, certain filters must be removed and replaced with faith, determination and a willingness to accept it and to take the next step towards deliverance from those things that the lack of truth hindered you from possessing. The goal of dealing with the true matters of your heart is for you to obtain a true breakthrough from all of the things that prevent you from being your best ordained self. Just as the people in **Acts 2:37** were pricked in their hearts, sometimes getting the real truth will unavoidably prick your heart before it repositions your heart upright. Truth is the tool designed to bring you into liberty. Truth isn't the enemy. It helps you to overcome the enemy's plot. Remember, facing the truth is the prerequisite to all of your sustainable deliverances.

This is book is an aid to help you to understand that you must become free and maintain your status of liberty. Don't lose sight of the value of emancipation. You must maintain your liberation after you're freed from thoughts, pain, rejection, abuse, sin, wounds or whatever's blocking your ordained progress. Unfortunately, the freedom gained from God can be lost. Losing it is not God's desire. I beg you to hold on to the new independence that you'll gain.

Galatians 5:1 tells us to *"Stand fast therefore in the liberty wherewith Christ hath made us free, and be not entangled again with the yoke of bondage."* Christ has made obtaining liberty possible; however, everyone who obtains it from Him is still told to stand fast in it and not to be found entangled in bondage again.

Embrace and invest...

It takes a personal investment of faith, time in prayer, reading the Word and obeying it to become free from strongholds and mindsets attached to matters that you have endured or are currently facing. It's time to embrace new victories and experience the God-reality life that He has for you! It's not only possible to obtain liberty; it's also possible to maintain the possession of your liberation. However, you must keep your heart in agreement with God's order for your life to do so.

You must invite God into your heart. Equally so, you must put your heart in God. Your heart needs to be fully submitted into God's hands, His will and His way. God being in your heart and your heart being in God are both vital and two incredibly different things. There must be an agreement of oneness between you and God. Learn to love what God loves and to hate what God hates. These things are easy to find, because they're located throughout the pages of the whole Bible. Learn to embrace them and learn them. Abide in them. Give His leading full reign in your heart. I would not be exercising full transparency if I didn't say that to do this takes a willing and determined heart. It's easier said than done, and it takes daily practice. It's a lifestyle of liberty.

Inviting God to work on the matters of your heart without having a willingness to submit your whole heart to Him only results in you receiving a lesser outcome than what God intended for you. Refusing to fully embrace God's way makes the benefit of being led by His Spirit and His Word of no effect. Adhering to your own way could be the cause that landed you in a place where His help was needed in the first place. Conversely, it could be that life has thrown so many punches at you that you finally realized that facing these matter God's way is the way that will lead you to triumph. God's ways aren't like your ways, so neither will the outcomes He brings be like any of the outcomes you could gain on your own. God's way is and will always be the better way, and that's putting it mildly.

I've already made my confession, but in case you missed it, the abbreviated version is I lived a half-hearted life for years. This is still a reality in some areas, sad to say. I'm definitely a work in progress that's being worked on daily. I recognize that the heart is a sponge and easily influenced by what enters into it. The truth is that the heart has the ability to enlarge itself in love and in hate, in joy and in sadness, in good and in evil. The heart needs a daily search by the Word and truth about the matters it faces to reveal what's in there.

I've had countless conversations with others who validate that I'm not alone in this understanding. Others have humbly admitted that they, too, are on a search to embrace the fullness of what God has for them. They, too, are in pursuit of the truth that *"maketh free."* I know, as a person on this same quest, that obtaining a better life starts with a true assessment of my heart, your heart and any heart connected directly or indirectly to you, an assessment that's more than a feeling about something or someone. That assessment must be based upon God's truth.

Making those assessments requires a personal investment. Invest the time needed to examine your heart. Do it now, even as you read the pages of this book. I guarantee that if you're honest with yourself, you'll see the hidden treasures of your heart revealed. Be ready for the priceless experience of a changed outlook on life forever. This book is loaded with many reiterations. That isn't a mistake, it's intentional. You're reminded repeatedly to free your heart from all deceptions by letting God's truth reveal the real matter. It's important that you understand that God can't be deceived. His eyes can't be shut. Nothing can be hidden from Him. There isn't a place within or without us that's unseen by His eyes or unknown by Him. Even the secret places are open to Him.

The psalmist wrote this revelation in **Psalms 139:1-12.** I believe it's worth taking the time to review, so let's do it now. It states,

"O LORD, thou hast searched me, and known me.

Thou knowest my downsitting and mine uprising, thou understandest my thought afar off.

Thou compassest my path and my lying down, and art acquainted with all my ways.

For there is not a word in my tongue, but, lo, O LORD, thou knowest it altogether.

Thou hast beset me behind and before, and laid thine hand upon me.

Such knowledge is too wonderful for me; it is high, I cannot attain unto it.

Whither shall I go from thy spirit? Or whither shall I flee from thy presence?

If I ascend up into heaven, thou art there: if I make my bed in hell, behold, thou art there.

If I take the wings of the morning, and dwell in the uttermost parts of the sea; Even there shall thy hand lead me, and thy right hand shall hold me.

If I say, Surely the darkness shall cover me; even the night shall be light about me.

Yea, the darkness hideth not from thee; but the night shineth as the day: the darkness and the light are both alike to thee."

My, my, my! This is an awesome reminder. Knowing that God sees it all should make you simultaneously very happy and very afraid. It should bring happiness knowing that God sees everything concerning you, he sees it all. It should make you a little afraid for the same reason: God sees it all! There's nothing that He doesn't already know about you. Every secret of your heart is open to Him. Some secrets about you remain secrets even to you until God reveals them.

God is unequivocally the revealer of secrets. He knows all secrets, those of your friends and enemies, yours and mine. God already knows the answer, unlike the man who has to seek God for answers. Whatever the problem is, it's never veiled to God; therefore, the solution is never veiled, either. God is able to reveal and decode the secrets. God exposing these is undoubtedly to your benefit.

Daniel 2:47 states, *"The king answered unto Daniel, and said, Of a truth it is, that your God is a God of gods, and a Lord of kings, and a revealer of secrets, seeing thou couldest reveal this secret."* These are the words spoken by a king. These words were spoken to Daniel after he was able to reveal to the king the secret that no one else could. Daniel could do it because he sought God for it. God gave him the secret and its revelation. Daniel invested time in prayer. He invested time to inquire of God concerning the matter. In return, God gave him what men couldn't figure out on their own. Daniel received knowledge as a result of seeking God that the others were unable to obtain by their own abilities, talents or gifts.

Seeking God may not be the first step that comes to mind to obtain answers for things. That doesn't surprise me, and it probably doesn't surprise most people. Seeking God must be intentional. You have to decide that you'll seek God about every issue and every matter, whether for a business decision, matters in your personal life, relationships, serving in ministry or just living life in general. Learn to give God free intervention to speak into your whole life. Be awakened to the truth that your heart is full of secrets: not just cute little harmless secrets either, but secrets that play the silent partner role in the everyday choices and decisions that you're making. These secrets are boldly or subtly a part of all of your actions.

Think about it. A secret isn't something that's openly disclosed. A secret quietly resides although it hasn't been identified or revealed to you. Not knowing of it doesn't make it a nonissue or nonexistent. God doesn't need a decoder, but everyone else does. We need help to unmask the hidden thing so we can see the unobvious truths. God is credited with being the source who reveals secrets in the Book of Daniel. Many other sources besides God attempt to provide insight, but they fail in comparison. I know this, because the Book of Daniel reflects it, as you'll see next. These other sources fail because they can be deceived themselves. God can't be deceived. God can't be deceived. Saying this repeatedly isn't a typo. God can't be deceived. Here's what's written in **Daniel 2:27-28**.

"Daniel answered in the presence of the king, and said, The secret which the king hath demanded cannot the wise men, the astrologers, the magicians, the soothsayers, shew unto the king;

But there is a God in heaven that revealeth secrets, and maketh known to the king Nebuchadnezzar what shall be in the latter days.

Thy dream, and the visions of thy head upon thy bed, are these;"

If you read further, you would see that Daniel proceeded to share the details of the king's secret to the king as it was revealed to him (Daniel) by God. The king credits Daniel for being accurate. Consistent, accurate and on-point revelation comes from God alone. He will show it to those who seek Him in truth. We read from **Psalms 139** earlier in this book. When you consider all of the things the psalmist mentioned in that psalm that God sees, it tells you that there is nothing hidden from Him. There isn't a matter that you have that escapes His knowing. There isn't a matter that He can't resolve. Let Him help you come to a real resolution for the real matters that are going on within your heart.

Real truth, real change ...

Change? Did you say, "Change"? Yes, as a matter of fact, I said, "Real change." Real truth will bring about a real change. Your perceptions will change when your heart is changed. Your outlook on life will change when your heart is changed. Deliverance will be yours when your heart is changed. You'll see life differently as your heart is kept upright before God.

The catalyst to all of these changes is truth. Truth isn't necessarily what you think it is. Truth is what actually "is". God knows the condition of the heart better than anyone else. He knows motives, intents, thoughts and aspirations. He knows everything about what lies within you. No matter how you may view yourself, what God sees of you is right, accurate and the truth. Once you see yourself through God's eyes -- and I want to make clear here that I'm not referring to how others see you but how God sees you based on His Word – and you can see past your filters into the reconciled place that God desires for you, please let Him plant His reality in you. Make His truth your truth and His reality for you your reality from this time forward.

This revelation served as a key that changed my life. It freed me up the day I understood it and has kept me moving forward on my Christian journey ever since. It unchained me from so many fetters, manacles, strongholds, limitations, restraints and barriers that were both visible and invisible to me. Understanding what God did for me gives me joy each time I think about it, when I remember that it's one of the things guaranteed to always cause my heart to strongly sing its song of praise to God! I believe that it would be a key for you if you understand this, just as it was and is for me, a key to the new life that you'll live starting today. This will have a riveting effect impressed upon you until your departing day from this earth. This was the impact that truth brought to me and to the others who have shared that they followed this pattern and experienced the same.

Well, you may be wondering, what is it? It's this, plain and simple: Once you see who you are through God's eyes, who you are based on God's Word and the promises of God for you, then stick with that alignment. That was a simple statement; however, don't read over it without lending thought to it. Adhere to and hold fast to the alignment that brought you into your revitalized status by God's revealed truth. Okay, here's an even simpler statement: Embrace the correction, rending, repairing, rebuking, uprooting, and the healing, compassion, forgiveness, restoration and new beginnings that truth brought you face to face to see – all of it! Embrace all that God's Word and the Holy Spirit have to reveal to you to bring you to the place of purging. Embrace all of it, because all of it is purposed to be the vehicle that will bring you into an upright position with God's will for you, so take it all in whole-heartedly!

Let the washing and the regeneration, the redemption – all of it – do what it was designed to do for you and for your good. Let it transform you from a place of disorder to order, from brokenness to wholeness, from sin to salvation, from darkness to light, from confusion to clarity, and from torn places to healed places.

Whatever deliverances you need, whatever breakthroughs are needed for you to walk in this life freed from the burdens of the unresolved matters in your heart, be ready to receive that deliverance. Everyone needs some relief of some kind, and receiving it will take heart work, so let the Spirit of God start this process in your heart.

I caution you that the process will be a threshing floor experience. I caution you so that you'll endure. Whatever you do, please don't quench this part of the process. This part of the process is a genuine work of the Holy Spirit. It will seem hard. Okay, it will be hard for a moment. It will seem time consuming and at times irrelevant to go through such a process at first, but stick with it. You'll see the fruit of your new beginning flourish time after time again.

It's very humbling to face things that have been planted and buried so deeply and maybe for so long. The process of renewal and deliverance strips off layers within you like nothing else.

Let it happen. It will definitely create a disturbance in you. Protecting you from disturbing these dormant layers is the heart's subconscious way of defending itself… at least that's what the heart believes prior to the process that will yield the awesome and refined fruit.

Here is my disclaimer before I go further. I'm not a doctor in any shape, form or fashion. I don't serve in any facet of the mental health profession. I don't hold a degree in psychology, and I'm not speaking as a subject matter expert when I say that the heart has layers that must be uncovered. However, I'm accurate in my conclusion about this: I boldly say that the heart has so many layers to it that must be uncovered, and because there are so many layers, it can cover up so many things. The heart is full of so many unknowns, even to you, its carrier.

The heart possesses many matters that aren't normally addressed. I proclaim this boldly not based upon a degree or even by some whim. I base this on what's written in **Jeremiah 17:9-10**. Take a moment to read what's written in this text by Jeremiah as it describes the heart itself. Keep in mind as you review the description of the heart that the heart doesn't have to remain in this state. Thank God for that! The heart is pliable, which means it can be turned, changed, injured, healed, be loving, cruel, full of light or full of darkness. Your heart can be a carrier of any of these, but how it remains depends upon you, its carrier.

Scriptural reference from **Jeremiah 17:9-10**

Matters of the Heart

"The heart is deceitful above all things, and desperately wicked: who can know it?

I the Lord search the heart, I try the reins, even to give every man according to His ways, and according to the fruit of His doings."

I referred to the threshing floor experience because I experienced my own version of it. I was seeking God through a hardship. I wasn't seeking to give up or to ask Him to release me from what I was experiencing. I've learned to suffer through those things. Longsuffering is among those named as fruits of the Spirit according to **Galatians 5:22-21.** I'm not a fan of longsuffering any more than the next person. However, I understand that it's a part of the walk of faith I chose. It comes with the territory, and I know that I draw nigh to hear what God is teaching me in the suffering. I repent of the things He shows me that I need to; I fight for the things He tells me to fight through, and I stand until He orders me to stand down, because that's what servants and soldiers do. They wait on their orders and work to fulfill them, so I wasn't trying to avoid any battle I was going through because I trust God.

This season of the threshing floor was transformational in a different way, a way that was new to me. It was working to remove something out of me while simultaneously breaking things away from me. I had to stay close to God's Word. I had to pray day and night and night and day, because as long as I was doing these things, he was doing that, and I didn't want Him to stop. There was a constant pull on my heart during this time. All I could do was yield. The more I submitted and yielded, the more truth spoke and the brighter the light that shined within.

The light brought revelation. The revelation brought me face to face with my heart. You would have thought that this would be a comfortable thing for me. It was great … and it was crushing. It was great, because I was beginning to understand why things were as they were in me and in my life. Ironically, it was crushing for the exact same reason. It was the encounters of truth. Truth sometimes brought me gladness and crushed me at other times.

The crushing is what I entitled my threshing floor experience. You may have heard of the threshing floor process, which is used by those who harvest wheat. The process is performed to separate the chaff from the wheat. A separation is needed because the chaff is designed to cover the wheat in its growing season, but it's the wheat kernel that must ultimately come forth, so the chaff must be broken off. The chaff is the outer part of the wheat that's seen until it's time to reveal the real inner value, which is the kernel. The kernel is within and can't be seen until the chaff has been removed.

The process of separating the chaff from the kernel is needful but somewhat brutal. Separating the chaff from the kernel isn't as simple as peeling off the chaff. The chaff has covered the kernel for so long that it's solidly fixed. It takes a violent crushing of the chaff for it to release the kernel. At this point the chaff must encounter a force that demands its release of the kernel.

The threshing floor is where it all happens. The threshing floor must be conducive to meeting the mandates required to help achieve this separation of chaff and wheat. The threshing floor isn't meant to be a nice comfortable place. It's not a safe haven or a warm place where the kernel could be gently coached to find its way out. It's quite the opposite. It's an uncomfortable, hard place, a cushion-less floor where the chaff is ground over repeatedly. This goes on for as long as it takes to break off the chaff and extract the kernel. The better the crushing, the better the chance of breaking the chaff away.

This is exactly how my threshing floor experience felt: Although it was a breakthrough for my heart, it was a crushing of my ways. It was rough. In this analogy, I felt as if I, my true self, was the kernel. Everything that was hiding my true self or my true value was the chaff. Uncovering my heart called for breaking away those things that were covering me up.

Let's just take a moment to look at what I mean when I say that there were many things that were covering me. I can probably write another whole book on the coverings that had to be broken off of me. Remember, the cause for the covering in the first place was to protect the wheat kernel as it grew. The chaff's work was fulfilled at the time of harvesting, and then it was time to break the chaff's grip and to extract the kernel. It's the kernel that has the real value, not the chaff.

The coverings weren't one specific thing in my case. My chaff was mingled with a number of things all wrapped up in one, and all were gripping my kernel. It was the "go along to get along mindset," the playing down of my heart's loyalty to God to be accepted by others, the trying not to be the "bull in the china shop" when all I could see was red from the china shop being filled with things that minimized the true Spirit of God. Seeing these things made a mockery of fearing and honoring God. Watching things that were contrary to God's will flow freely and being justified by religious and worldly clichés like "God knows my heart," "Nobody's perfect," "God understands" and many more like these just ate me up inside.

The problem wasn't that the clichés were untrue. The problem wasn't even the cliché itself but the context in which they were being used most of the time. They always seemed to come about conveniently to justify an action that should have been repented. These clichés always seemed to have been an escape of accountability, a replacement of standing in faith, a justification for disobeying the Word, an excuse for not standing on God's promises, or simply a disregard of honoring God over the failing desires of the flesh.

My chaff was in wrestling with the politics I had to perform to maintain, as much as possible, the status of living peaceably with all. The adjustment I was making to appear approachable to people who didn't exemplify, through their actions, my same core values. I genuinely like people. Sometimes my core beliefs will cause me to refrain from participation in certain things that are labeled harmless by others. However harmless they may be to others these things may not align with what I believe. That doesn't make me right or righteous. It makes me who I am, just as others' differences make them who they are.

Stay with me on this. I'm being transparent and promise that I'm going to come to the point shortly. Choosing to abide in your faith by not participating in some of the things that others choose to partake in will give the appearance that you're partial to people. The truth may be that you're not partial to people so much as you're just not interested in participating in some of the things that they've chosen to participate in.

I learned in hindsight that when you find yourself in the position of looking like an outcast or one whose ways are the least preferred, you're not always in a position to explain yourself in your effort to avoid being misunderstood. Unfortunately, it isn't uncommon to be misunderstood, a situation that isn't isolated just to me. This goes for anyone. Misunderstanding occurs and errors in judgment are likely made when people don't understand the heart of others. Judging the book by its cover can cause anyone to err. It has caused me to err many times. I will not speak for you on this; I remain transparent and vulnerable in sharing that I've repented many times for doing this. I still have to consciously remind myself daily to stay clear of judging a book by its cover.

I had apparently developed a nice, strong, healthy outer shell prior to God dealing with me so strongly in this area. My chaff was high quality. It was there to protect me as I was growing. It had served to help me in minimize the awkwardness I often experienced and it lessened the possibility of being misunderstood … well at least it did, sometimes. The truth is that my chaff was aiding my efforts to try to be as "normal" as I could be according to other's definitions of "normality," just to be partially accepted sometimes.

I was covered in the chaff of trying to conform to whatever it took to live peacefully. I was doing simple things such as ensuring I looked at someone, greeting them at least with a head nod so they wouldn't think I was in a mood or being cold, when the truth was that I may have only had a few hours of sleep because I was up late doing something to help someone else have a better lifestyle, and what I was trying to do was take a moment to breath and get that one last "help me God" prayer so that my own flesh would be under subjection before greeting someone else. This approach sometimes failed, because in my haste to get this quick silent prayer in, my head nod was late and I was misunderstood again. Or if I was trying to be conscious enough to ensure I smiled at least once in an attempt to escape being labeled with one of the many labels that I'd repeatedly witnessed being placed on others, when, more than the need to generate a, let's just all get along smile, I needed to handle the thing that was blocking my authentic smile from naturally coming forth in the first place. I was working so hard trying to ensure, to the best of my ability, that I was exemplifying respect to everyone in every way possible by listening to others, sharing my true opinion when asked, and by staying in my lane. Trust me, people will let you know exactly where your lane is, so when they do, get in it and learn to love it. It's actually quite nice once you realize that staying in your lane releases you from having to focus all over the place. It's quite the gift when you think about it. I adapted as needed in an effort not to purposefully offend anyone, yet somehow, despite all my best efforts, I still managed to offend people anyway.

People deserve to be treated with courtesy, respect and brotherly love, not because they're mini-me's or that we have all things in common, but because they're human beings. Furthermore, they're God's workmanship. No matter how different we all are, we're all the same in that regard. We all have strengths and flaws. I'm not encouraging the notion that we should not make efforts to show love or attempt in every way to live harmoniously. I'm not promoting coldness, mean-spiritedness or solitude. However, you should never feel pressured to forfeit or exchange your commitment to remain authentic and loyal to your faith and to God simply to win the confirmation or validation of others, especially when the demands of obtaining other's favor require anything of you that will result in the reduction of or a falling away from the things that you're doing in an honest effort to please or serve God. Don't willingly compromise or do anything that will draw you further away from God, and be quick to repent if you do it in error. Whew! That was a mouth full.

The funny thing in looking back on what my outer shell was working so hard to protect, most of the time, is that nobody even paid those efforts any attention. No one pays chaff any attention. I also know "now" not to pay it any attention. I know now that the outer part isn't the most valuable part. The inner part holds the treasure. People make all of these subtle sacrifices for nothing. Others may not know or even care that you're making them because, first, they never asked you to make the sacrifices, and second, they're probably trying to do their best to maintain their own path. People don't know when you're making extra efforts or when these are genuine displays from your heart. Only God knows. So why try to please people when you can be your true self and have peace? Don't yoke yourself up with these types of useless burdens. That's chaff. Yes! This is enlightenment and liberty that's talking to you right now through the pages of this book. It took the breaking of many yokes to finally gain this inch of freedom. I refuse to return to bondage – at least, not on purpose! And I refuse to assist the blinders that seek to hinder you from your greater liberated life by withholding from you what I know has helped me.

These were my outward shells. These were the layers of chaff covering my wheat. These mindsets and concepts were burdening my heart, and God wanted to break me free. These strongholds and deceptions had to be broken. My true heart had to be dealt with, and it was right there on the threshing floor.

I felt under "pressure" during this threshing floor experience. The pressure was in the form of the brightest spotlight ever. This was no ordinary light, this light came with the presence of the Lord. It was like being under the eye of the big "G" God, the God of gods. The God who is Holy, Righteous, All-Powerful, All-Seeing, All-Knowing, All-Everything! This presence alone immediately taught me what was meant by the "fear of the Lord."

I felt inadequate, like the scum of the earth, because I could sense this outstanding presence of Holiness. I knew that all of my righteousness meant nothing in His presence. The only thing I was sure of in that moment was surely He is present, and He will not find anything good within me; no, nothing good at all. Everything I considered to be good in me vanished from my mind in His presence. My good efforts, my good attempts, my good intentions all appeared as dung; they were as nothing. I felt naked, stripped of all coverings, nothing was hidden in my mind, heart, spirit or soul. It felt as if the very presence of God was right there hovering over me, and all of my flaws were volunteering to show themselves to Him. They were all stepping up to the mic saying, "Here I am, and I surrender." Every bit of credibility I thought I possessed forsook me one by one. I couldn't help but to feel condemned. I thought, "God's absolutely not going to want anything to do with me after this." I was thinking that all of my ways must be the most detestable thing He's ever seen. Remember, He's God and He's seen it all, but in that moment I felt like I imagine Isaiah and Gideon might have felt when they had their encounter with God.

Truth had me surrounded and under arrest. The light of His presence brought undeniable truth: my truths, then God's truth, which were two very different truths, by the way. I could see clearly that God's truth is the truth, and reigns. I could see everything so clearly, and I was clearly a pure mess in the light. I definitely didn't meet any qualifying standards that would have granted me the privilege of receiving any of God's promises. All I can tell you is that it was rough, but I needed to see it. I was Mrs. "I'm trying to do the right thing toward all mankind Lord, so, help me out, please!" and, I needed to stay right there under the pressure of the light to see the truth about my heart's condition. The truth, the whole truth, and nothing but the truth, so help me God.

I had to see it and accept it. I wept because I didn't want to believe all of the truths about myself. I'm a "good person" was the way I had labeled myself. The truth wasn't saying that my core didn't possess some good. The truth was saying that my core had areas within it that needed deliverance just as every heart does, that hasn't been exposed and freed from its shortcomings. Remember, the heart is deceitful. It takes God to reveal its content. Even then, you have to take the "me" blinders off for a really good look at what's being revealed.

Things started to happen as I did that. Pride stood up and died. It literally gave up the ghost, because it couldn't withstand the truth process that I was undergoing at that time. Embracing truth will not only bring pride to its knees; it will also kill it and remove it from you if you let truth continue.

Oh, by the way, joy, which I'm quite fond of, seemingly grew wings and fled far away from me during this stripping process. When I couldn't find my joy anywhere in this process, I thought for certain depression was going to be the only thing waiting for me at the end of this. I was having a personal "woe is me, I'm undone" moment like Isaiah and my own version of "I'm not a vessel of valor" experience like Gideon had with His God encounter.

Think about it: I was experiencing all of this because I had pressed in by much praying as I'd been led to do. All of the reading of the Word, lifting up the hearts of all, including my own, to God. All of the crying out and longing for the will of

God to manifest for my life. I chose to open up to God and trust Him to show me what was in my heart, to show me the matters of my own heart. I wanted His truth because I wanted the fullness of walking in true reconciliation with Him – the Holy God.

As painful as this encounter was, revealing my pride and ego, I accepted the pain of facing my strongholds because I wanted true deliverance from the lies that were working against me and inside my heart. God gave me the courage to take the excuse filters away, the courage to peel back the filters of justifications, to take the walls down and to remove even the emotional filters that stood as faithful guards ready to "fix" me or "comfort" me before I could even see the brokenness that was in me.

I had to recognize that all of the filters that prevented truth were, in reality, blockers and barriers that were hindering or preventing me from being my best possible self. I realized that sometimes real breakthroughs are prevented from manifesting because the wounds are filtered.

I could suddenly see and understand that these filters were connected. Injury birthed fear. Fear birthed regret. Regret birthed failure, and the layers of filters and their negative impacts just kept piling up on one another, each filter hiding the injury, serving as a safeguarded, a bandage. The filters misrepresented themselves as bandages and coverings needed for healing. "Keep it covered until it heals." These weren't healing bandages, they were cover ups. These were the things I pronounced as healed to keep moving forward. They produced the smiles that covered the frowns, the laughter that covered the silent cries and the masks that covered the sadness that was hidden deep inside because I hadn't taken the time to thoroughly pray it all the way through. Underlined in my heart were good intentions that were generated to press forward; however, at some point, they had to be realized to be matters of my heart that would ultimately need to be undressed and faced to be healed. The light of the Gospel, the truth, heals. It doesn't appear to be the case at first, but neither does the surgeon's cut that's necessary, in some cases, to get you back to wholeness. This encounter with truth helped me to undress my heart before God. It allowed the loving kindness of God to heal known and unknown brokenness abiding in my heart's secrets, and boy, I'm so glad about it now!

I want to say this to you now. If you're experiencing any level of pain at all – not just physical pain, but emotional pain, such as disappointment, regret, rejection, resentment – realize this truth: The pain is coming from somewhere. Allow God to deal with you in that place for the purpose of healing. If you're angry, even if the anger is legitimate, let God's love and faithfulness move past the filters covering it right now to begin the healing process. Letting it be healed doesn't justify excusing the person who caused it, but it will help to relieve you from the burden of having to carry its weight. God still knows about it, and He is the faithful judge. Let God decide how He will judge matters that need judgement. If it's the judgement that you're concerned about before you can let the anger go, **Hebrews 10:30** says, *"For we know Him that hath said 'Vengeance belongeth unto me, I will recompense,' saith the Lord. And again, the Lord shall judge His people."* Recognize that the anger is holding on to something, and so is the fear, the lust, the depression, the doubt or whatever it may be that's deeply rooted in your heart.

Covering up what you know is there will never make it go away; it just sits there under layers and layers of the stuff that we justifiably pile up over it. It has to be uncovered to be properly assessed. I was guilty of misapplying the healing. I was conditioned to quickly speak the healing and move on. This was my quick claim and declaration of faith. I instantly spoke healing over whatever wound tried to surface. We are quick to do this, just like all fired up, sanctified, full-of-faith believers. I'm not suggesting that you not speak by faith. I'm suggesting that you tell the truth about it, as much as you know, in your prayer closet. Confess what lies within your heart to God. You can be healed of anything. The lesson I had to learn here is to refrain from quickly covering up the wound of a matter and never going back to remove the bandage to make sure it's healing. Let God unwrap it, deal with it and heal you from it. Don't stop at letting the wound be quickly wrapped and making that the only step. It's a start in the right direction. Some wounds do well under wrapping alone; others don't. Follow through in prayer and let the Great Physician heal it to the core.

I realized in hindsight that you can pray a general prayer asking for complete healing. You can't ask for specific healing in an area you never recognized was sick or injured. That would be like taking medicine for a sickness you were unaware you had. This happens all of the time, and the onset of this error is usually brought on by the self-guess work of self-diagnosing and self-treating. The problem with this method is, if you don't know the real problem, you're taking a big gamble at applying the right solution. You are beating at the air. You must let God show you what's present within and the damage it's causing to your overall well-being. Don't live a life in pain, because you do have another option. Don't live a half-hearted life – half of the heart enlightened and the other half left in darkness. Let God help you in every area of your life, in every area of your heart.

I eventually came to see that my filters were like brakes that I subconsciously pumped, and in doing so, I slowed down the progress that unfiltered truth would have quickly granted me. My filters kept sending me backwards. They were taking me out of God's assessment and putting me back into the realms of "Everything's great" and "I'm okay." Hallelujah! God had a better plan for me than to leave me to my own understanding! I'm glad that He shined His light into my heart, a light so bright that it revealed even the filters themselves.

Filters are unconscious laborers. They're busy at work in an attempt to guard your heart from truth, and they're operating in auto-pilot mode. Filters can only function in areas that you're unaware of or unintentional about. They're there to secure the acceptable norms. They can do this because they're familiar with your boundaries. They know the brightness of the regular and approved light. Filters are acquainted with your normalcy. Unfortunately, filters will work to hinder the greater light from disturbing the tolerable darkness and will sound the alarm when an attempt is made by the greater light. Pray and train your heart, mind and soul to let the light of God's truth and wisdom through. Filters can be and must be removed to receive greater enlightenment. The removal of the filters must be intentional. Pray these down in the presence of God during your prayer time. Ask God to replace the filters with strength, health and healing. Make sure the filters aren't being removed to allow more deception to enter in. Guard your heart from evil. **Proverbs 4:23** teaches *"Keep thy heart with all diligence; for out of it are the issues of life."*

Guard your heart from greater darkness. Let in the greater light. Fight the good fight in relieving your heart from things that prevent truth from being revealed to it. This isn't a self-guided process. Petition the help of the Holy Spirit, the Word, the wisdom of God, the armor of God – everything of God, nothing of flesh. The greater light referred to here is God's truth, not people's. We subconsciously or consciously filter our minds, our willingness to hear and our hearts. The truth doesn't reach the core when the light of the truth is filtered. The core is the depth. Yes, deep within my core there were things that hadn't been reached. Deep within my inner man were things that weren't reached. Deep within my heart were things that hadn't been revealed. There were things there that had laid dormant unknowingly. The same is true for you. How do I know? Because the same is true for every living man. The purging is perpetual, because every heart is every bit of what **Jeremiah 17:9** says it is: *"deceitful above all things, and desperately wicked."*

I've shared some fairly personal things. The reason I can talk about it so openly to the world without shame is because I understand the importance of sharing this message with others so they can receive real deliverance. I know that all filters aren't bad. Filters are put in place to block out the entrance of a specific thing that shouldn't have access. The filters I am referring to that should be removed are the self-placed filters that are put in place to keep self-thoughts in and block God's truth out. It will take the removal of these filters that block truth from doing a work even after the truth makes the real issue known by God's Word. No one wants to believe that they have any issues or any darkness at all within themselves. I didn't want to believe it about myself, either. I prided myself on always trying to do the right thing. It was crushing for my pride and hard for my soul to see me in the light God was revealing when what He was revealing, was actually good. It was eye opening for me to even accept that I had filters in places that were hindering God's truth from entering into the deep places of my heart. I was in denial. I know now that everyone will benefit by accepting the fact that there's something in all of our hearts that's not 100% on point with truth and God's ways. There's something in there that the light hasn't been fully permitted to shine on. This is why darkness exists and will continue to exist until the true light is allowed to enter in. Darkness? It sounds horrible and so wicked. It sounds so deceitful, right? Nobody wants to claim that, but it sounds just like the description the Bible gives for the heart. It sounds like the truth. The heart is deceitful and wicked, and it takes God to search it out. The heart is just being the heart, and no one knows the heart better than God.

This was a hard pill to swallow. The sobering moments are what helped me, the times God used to reveal His truth to me. His love and guidance were for my good. God's truth and the light it brings were indeed manifestations of His grace. That amazing grace! Grace was on the scene. It revealed His love, the agape love whose depth all the books in the world couldn't cover, so pure, so uncondemning that I trusted its truth and allowed it to travel anywhere within my heart that it desired, even to its depths.

Agape love is God's love. I understood that God's love wasn't there to injure but to heal. It wasn't there to constrain me but to set me free. It wasn't present to judge me harshly but to bring justice. I understood that God loves me so much that He speaks truth in my heart to drive out all deceptions, even those I never even wanted to admit were present. It was by His love that He took the filters off of the wound that was still present, though hidden, with "the promise to fully heal it.

God loves you that much, too! My joy is renewed just to write of His love. God's love isn't to be confused with the love that you receive from anyone or anything else. Not your closest friend, a family member, coworker, boss, teacher, spouse, child – or anyone! No one can compete with the love God gives. His love is like no other love, and if being the recipient of this great love wasn't enough, it comes with immeasurable benefits.

Thank God for His love and grace. Grace helped me see God's love, which helped me to trust God's light, which caused me to surrender my whole heart to God, which resulted in me letting the light of God's Word have free reign in my heart, uncaged, unguarded and with no filters before Him. God's truth could then reach my whole heart, its depths, heights, corners, crevices and crannies. God's love and grace taught me to remove filters that interfered with His progress for my life. I learned to let truth have at it, no matter how brutal it seemed at the moment, to let it happen and let it free my heart from whatever was there that needed to be released. This meant hearing truth, receiving truth, processing truth and allowing truth to do its work. And boy, did truth do a work in my heart!

Truth did what nothing else had been able to do or will ever be able to accomplish in me! Truth made me better, not bitter. Truth came with healing that didn't prematurely wrap the wound before assessing it. Truth set me free from the clutches of the guilt and shame that accompanied it after I completed the orders that came with it. Truth brought me to a new place of liberty. Hallelujah! That's my testimony.

I crave truth now. I'm not a glutton for punishment; however, I appreciate the help in matters of my heart. I find that now I'm somewhat offended when I recognize that something other than truth is operating for or against me. I would rather have truth in operation that leaves me temporarily disappointed than to have deception in operation that leaves me believing I had accomplished something when I actually had failed. Truth isn't easy to hear; however, as I've experienced, truth heals its own wounds and others' wounds. I find that I heal with truth. Besides, if I didn't know I had failed and if truth never revealed it, I may never have had the opportunity to at least attempt to truthfully succeed at the thing I failed. I hope that makes sense, because I sincerely meant that.

We can be nice, cordial, professional, friendly and so forth; we should all practice and embrace these great behaviors.

However, being these things alone doesn't mean deception isn't present. Don't think outward niceness is proof that all is well in your heart. Many people can go along to get along, but it's possible that their heart isn't with you. **Proverbs 23:7** tells us, *"For as he thinketh in His heart, so is he: Eat and drink, saith he to thee; but His heart isn't with thee."* This reference proves that honesty is a greater virtue than niceness, so be honest with yourself and with others. Exterior behaviors are great, but it takes more than exterior behaviors to be delivered from interior strongholds.

Be authentic. Be you even when you're not accepted by others. Be you even if you have lack and need deliverance. Be the real you. It's a challenge I still fight daily to overcome. Don't fake it until you make it; instead, let truth do its work in you. Trust the work of truth, and you'll be authentically thankful when your deliverance is a reality.

It is refreshing to be free from these thoughts and emotions, with no airs, no conceit, no deception and no masquerades. This is the awesome gift that God gives through truth. **John 8:32** says, *"And ye shall know the truth, and the truth shall make you free."* You shall know it, and as a result of knowing it, you shall be made free by it. That sweet, sweet freedom awaits you right on the other side of the light. So, let the light shine in.

Don't forfeit ...

There's more. Yes, there is more good news. I shared the threshing floor experience and its purpose to remove the outward exterior to get to the core. I shared how facing realities is part of the work that releases the grip of the thing preventing your true liberty. Getting rid of the chaff by way of the threshing process is only part of the journey. I shared how you must let God's Word do a real work in your heart; I mean, let the truth of God have at it. Seriously, let truth do its ministry unfiltered. You be in alignment with God's will for your life at the end of it all. The truth will reposition you, restore you, refresh you – all of that. No matter how hard the ripping may seem, truth will leave you whole at the conclusion.

The details of my process aren't to deter you from wanting to go through with your own deliverance. Stay open. Encountering truth produces a God-ordained and intense process, but it's all good! **Hebrews 4:12** *states, "For God's Word is quick, and* *powerful, and sharper than any two-edged sword, piercing even to the dividing asunder of soul and spirit, and of the joints and marrow, and is a discerner of the thoughts and intents of the heart."*

God's Word is the truth that's likened to that which is sharper than the sharpest sword. I was working with a paper cutter once. I lifted the handle to position the stack of papers. In pushing the papers up to the bar, the back of my hand barely touched the blade on the lifted handle. It barely tapped the handle's blade, yet it nipped the back of my hand. I was ok, but I was surprised that it took no force from my hand or the handle to be cut because the blade was just that sharp. God's Word isn't compared to a paper cutter but to a sword. Not just a sword but the sharpest two-edged sword, and the sharpness of the Word is said to be even sharper than that.

This tells me that the truth is so sharp that only application, not force, is needed for it to cut. **Ephesians 4:15** starts by saying, *"But speaking the truth in love."* Love is how truth should be delivered. Please don't confuse the phrase "in love" to mean that the delivery of truth will not ruffle any feathers. Speaking the truth "in love" doesn't imply that the delivery of the truth will be painless. Truth is so powerful and sharp that a slight brush against it will cut. It will ruffle feathers with no manly force applied because it's strong on its own. It can't be assumed that the sharing of truth will not cause pain, and when it does, it doesn't mean it wasn't delivered in love. It's not a lack of love to speak straight to the true matter at hand. It's not brutal to tell the truth or to be told the truth.

I know that cutting through hidden layers of untruths, masked façades and protective gear sounds brutal. God isn't being brutal when he opens up the heart with this tool called truth. As you read in **Hebrews 4:12**, God's Word involves piercing and dividing, surpassing exterior forms; looking into the soul and the spirit; searching the bones; discerning thoughts; and even knowing the heart's intent! Truth goes deep because things can hide well in the deep. Things are buried in the depths. The scripture referenced getting to the bone. Many layers are disturbed in getting to the bone.

Once the benefits of truth are rightly applied in love and the amazing results are gained from its application, then truth will be better appreciated and seen in its association with love. Love isn't brutal. It also doesn't have to be passive in its presentation to be validated as true love. The heart of truth works in conjunction with the heart of love. Both desire freedom for you. The hearts of truth and love desire that all the forces of untruths that are present to rob you of all levels of victory are expelled far away from you.

Here's the good thing, the part that many who are seeking new life, joy, restoration, peace and salvation will unfortunately forfeit. I urge you not to join those who have forfeited their breakthrough and lost all of the great progress they had gained.

Don't forfeit it all away after enduring the stripping away of darkness, being enlightened, and after being corrected, being rebuked, encountered with truth through love and having received the amazing grace of God and whatever the process of realignment took to get you free. It's a sad outcome to leave deliverance at the table and just walk away. It's like leaving the threshing floor with no wheat kernel when this happens. Some walk away from the victory because they simply didn't choose to live out of the redeemed heart, the heart that was made upright and restored by truth.

Many never embrace this important truth, the truth that the end result of addressing the matters of the heart leaves it whole. **John 3:17** tells us, *"For God sent not his Son into the world to condemn the world; but that the world through him might be saved."* Leave with the benefit. Don't miss this powerful revelation. It changed my life! It's another key that will change yours, no mistake about it. I mentioned when I shared my threshing floor experience how bad I felt in that process. I genuinely felt broken. I likened it to chaff being separated from the kernel, a crushing process.

The important point I have to make clear is this: Although I felt crushed, God never allowed the crushing to destroy me. I wasn't the target of destruction in this process. Please understand this. God doesn't intend to destroy you, either. This is a process of true redemption, though it may appear at times that God is angry with you or that he is rejecting you. It may feel this way because of the way He deals with you. He deals with you with a truth so pure that it almost seems brutal. It cuts, pierces and divides. Know that God never ever despises you, not in the least, and he never will. He loves you! I realize this time and time again. God is love. Thank goodness for that!

All of the pruning, purging, stripping, correcting and revealing that I mentioned in agony was meant to surface the hidden matters within my heart. You must acknowledge it. It was painful to face, but God wasn't making it a painful process on purpose. The purpose of pulling all of the darkness up out of your heart and showing it to you is to allow you the opportunity to confess that it was there and to admit that it was present in your heart. However, after seeing what was there blocking you from His best outcome for you and acknowledging that it was there, you were to be godly sorrowful[1] for it, which should have led you to repentance. Paul said this in **2 Corinthians 7:10**, *"For godly sorrow worketh repentance to salvation not to be repented of."* The intent was for you to sincerely choose to turn from the darkness that He revealed that was residing within you and, to follow His leading to freedom by the light of grace that was present to deliver you from all of the strongholds that were attached to the darkness, ultimately setting you free by the truth that dispelled the darkness. In short, liberation is the goal of God's truth.

You're expected to whole-heartedly and actually receive the true deliverance it brings after the truth is revealed and you have renounced the parts that weren't in alignment with God's Word. That's good, but that's still not all of it. Once you reach a victory, the expectation was and still is – that you walk, no – live in that victory!

This is the main key. You are to live the rest of your life in the new place of deliverance. Sounds simple enough, but don't underestimate this statement. It has unlocking, yoke-breaking power. Here it is again: You're to actually live out your redeemed life redeemed! This should cause your joy to be full and running over right now.

This yoke-breaking truth is so liberating! Just knowing it will strengthen your relationship with God. I've grown spiritually wiser from this insightful truth. Understanding this is also a real weapon against the adversary and a real victory for those who embrace it. The enemy can't hold you bound to living out of a heart condition that no longer exists. There's no reason you should revert to living from the demands of the old things that have been stripped away if the old heart has been changed and made new through God's process. There's no way you can continue to live out of the old heart without forfeiting the deliverance that truth has brought forth.

---

1. "godly sorrow," Blueletterbible.org, accessed August 26, 2020, https://www.blueletterbible.org/Comm/guzik_david/StudyGuide2017-2Cr/2Cr-7.cfm?a=1085010

Walking in the newness of life...

God gave you the awesome ability to choose to make life changes happen! You have that ability right now, so "let" it happen. Live out of that new heart immediately after it's renewed! Live from the redeemed heart the minute it's redeemed! Choose to live out of that upright heart, the heart that God has made upright! I urge you with excitement to understand that you're not a prisoner to the heart that was injured through rejection or abuse. No, you're not endlessly bound to the heart that was marred by hardships or the heart that was wounded by abandonments or mangled by life's shipwrecks. Don't live enslaved to the heart that was torn and darkened. Instead, live healed and enlightened! Believe that truth does exactly what God says it does: It makes you free. God's Word of truth freed you from the old heart as you turned your heart to align with His leading and chose to walk according to His Word because, the truth mightily drives out the darkness by its light!

No matter how it may continue to feel, the truth is that you brought your heart to face the things that were hindering your growth. You were released from the strongholds that once held you captive through deceit. This is the reality of your transformation as you yielded to God. Don't forsake your faith in God's Word; instead, let that truth liberate you into a life that's more abundant. The same way that you walked in deception unknowingly due to the lack of light, now walk away from the deception, wickedness, rejection, and darkness with your God-given redemption by choosing to live out of the heart that was repositioned upright through true repentance. God gave you a heart that's reconciled to Him by and through Christ Jesus. You can now live out of that reconciled heart. This is wonderful to know and even better to experience.

2 Corinthians 5:17-18 says, *"Therefore if any man be in Christ, he is a new creature: old things are passed away; behold, all things are become new. And all things are of God, who hath reconciled us to himself by Jesus Christ, and hath given to us the ministry of reconciliation."* The "all things" in the text includes your heart. It's time to take the brakes off of your redemption's claim. The light is green, go forward now redeemed. Once the matters are addressed and God has provided you the remedy of deliverance, it's time to forsake the old and behold the new. It's time to live out of that "delivered" heart.

Enlightenment peeled back the darkness. What great news! You still must choose to walk in the light. You never have to return to serving the demands of that old heart nor its fruits again. Embrace the change. Walk in the newness of life. Don't let anyone prevent you from living it out by their lack of understanding of what God did in bringing you to a real place of overcoming the obstacles that were working against you by half truths.

You can continue letting God's Word do a greater work in your heart with every single matter. Make your heart God's continuous workshop. Let Him teach you to manage the matters of your heart by bringing them to Him. Let truth bring you the best possible outcome in life. Why wait? Start being free today! Once free, strive to stay free. Remain honest with yourself and with God.

Ask the Father to help you ...

I'm the one sharing how awesome the gift of liberty is, but make no mistake about it, the experience of liberty I received wasn't one that I self-generated. It was by grace, prayer and the reading and hearing of God's Word. This process wasn't something I concocted or conjured up. I'm a recipient of God's grace and love. He receives all of the glory for the things He has done, is doing and will do in my life. I unashamedly give acknowledgement to God. I boldly profess that I'm a Christian and that God is my help. You've already witnessed me talking about God in the course of this book. You've seen me talking about Jesus and the help of the Holy Spirit. Rightly so, because the grace of God isn't masked. There's no pursuit of self-credibility. I shared a remedy God uses to break the heart out of its chains of wickedness and deception, a remedy proven to me. I bear its fruit in my life. It's not complicated at all, it's simple. God helped me to see how important it is to not take matters into your own hands but to bring your matters to Him.

I want you to let God help you find the next level of breakthrough in life. I know that He will because He is no respecter of persons. Our needs aren't the same. I understand that. Maybe your experience will be different because your needs are different. Maybe my strongholds are different than yours, and your strongholds are nothing like mine at all. Maybe your darkness or the things that you're failing to see in yourself aren't the same as the faults I saw in me or the faults you saw in me as I shared my story. Maybe we differ even in perception or the way I expressed myself throughout the pages ... maybe, maybe, maybe; the "maybe" list can go on and on. One thing I know for sure, though, is that you have needs.

I know you have strongholds and that you have darkness in you. I can say this with surety because you have sin in you. You have strongholds, darkness and faults because these things accompany sin. This statement isn't me being judgmental, this statement is based upon scripture. **Romans 3:23** *states, "All have sinned, and come short of the glory of God."* **Ecclesiastes 7:20** *says, "For there is not a just man upon earth, that doeth good, and sinneth not."* These two scriptures alone indicate that no one is exempt from strongholds, faults and sin; therefore, everyone needs to be freed from these things and the results they manifest. Everyone is a candidate for deliverance from the untruths that blind our eyes, deafen our ears and confuse our hearts by way of some type of darkness.

I've obeyed the Holy Spirit's leading and wrote this book just as I was pressed to do. I want you to know that there's an urgency from the Father in this ordained moment to free you from all of the antics and tactics opposing His will for your life. I've shared enough for you to know that the enemy's trick is to leave you in the dark, but God's grace is to send forth the light that will drive the darkness away.

You know for yourself, whether you'll admit it or not, that you've tried to break free in areas of your life and in areas of your thinking that you've been unable to successfully break away from. The prevention of this victory lies within a stronghold, a stronghold within you. The stronghold is opposing your liberation in that area. You have been unable to break free on your own because it requires a truth you've been unwilling to receive... a truth that will shatter the yoke once your whole heart is surrendered to God.

The power needed to break whatever strongholds you may face is in God's Word, in receiving it, believing it and living it! There are many smart, wise, strong and lovable people on the earth, but none smarter, wiser, stronger or more loving than God our Creator and the Maker of all. His love covers and recovers. Love is designed to redeem. **1 Peter 4:8** states, *"And above all things have fervent charity among yourselves; for charity shall cover the multitude of sins."* Love seeks not to condemn but to save.

Many approaches can be taken in hopes of receiving breakthroughs, but there's no true victory without God. There's no true way of living a life as ordained by your maker without His help. There's nothing I can share of myself that will produce a power strong enough to break any stronghold; we both know this. In fact, you can't gain your authentic internal freedom from anyone else except through Jesus Christ, the Son of God!

Standing on the Word ...

The scriptural reference used earlier, **Romans 3:23**, stated in part that everyone had *"sinned and come short"*. The shortness signifies that the way to an authentic breakthrough isn't obtained by us. Deliverance isn't granted or obtained through or by other people because everyone came short. Think about it this way, you were unable to achieve your own breakthrough on your own is because you were a part of the matter that prevented the breakthrough from manifesting. Actually, it was the sin within that was allowed to reside that kept you bound to the darkness. I know that this statement might be another one of those statements that seem insensitive or a little prickly, however, it's a true statement. Either you put the filters up to prevent the light of truth from coming into your heart and/or you were enlightened indeed but chose not to come out of that which you were enlightened of, leaving you in the darkness by choice. These strong statements are not made to bring condemnation or an accusation. God's Word explains it below in the scriptural reference from **John 3:19-21**. The choice is always yours to either take the path of light or chose to remain in the dark. **John 3:19-21** says, *"And this is the condemnation, that light has come into the world, and men loved darkness rather than light, because their deeds were evil. For everyone that doeth evil hateth the light, neither cometh to the light, lest his deeds should be reproved. But he that doeth truth cometh to the light, that his deeds may be made manifest, that they are wrought in God."* Amen! This is the real solution to the real problem.

You and I are reconciled from sin and from darkness back to God by Christ. **2 Corinthians 5:21** teaches, *"For he hath made him to be sin for us, who knew no sin; that we might be made the righteousness of God in him."* The "he" in this text is Christ. The deficiency isn't in Christ; it's resolved through Him. Jesus is the way that the Father made to redeem man back to Himself; this was the reason for His birth. **2 Corinthians 5:19** says, *"To wit, God was in Christ, reconciling the world unto himself, not imputing their trespassed unto them; and hath committed unto us the word of reconciliation."* You can't embrace part of the truth; you must accept the whole truth. Whole truth is where true deliverance lies.

I can't deliver you. You can't deliver me. We can't deliver anyone. My inability to deliver you or the inability of anyone else to deliver you into your place of breakthrough should not be a disappointment. The producer of your reconciliation to wholeness only comes by the way that God established. He deals with the heart of man. Anything else or any other way will either fail or serve to be a temporary victory at best.

I say, with the greatest humility and respect towards all, that God's Word is the light. I know there are other beliefs. I know there are other doctrines that others believe in strongly. Not to be argumentative, but my faith does not waver, neither will I apologize for referencing God's Word as the truth, because I believe it's the infallible truth. I've shared scriptures and will continue to share them throughout this book. Scriptures give light and instructions to those attempting to reach God's ordained destinations. They correct wrongs, perfect imperfections and give direction. **2 Timothy 3:16-17** states, *"All scripture is given by inspiration of God, and is profitable for doctrine, for reproof, for correction, for instruction in righteousness: That the man of God may be perfect, thoroughly furnished unto all good works."*

It's not my intention to offend anyone by the use of scriptures. I exercise and reserve the right to stand by my faith; therefore, I will not refrain from using scripture throughout the book. As I said, I understand that not everyone will agree with scripture or my interpretations of them. We have our differences and the Word even tells us how to deal with that. **Romans 14:5** says, *"One man esteemeth one day above the another: another esteemeth every day alike. Let every man be fully persuaded in His own mind."*

Pray. Ask God to direct your path and to bring you into the revelation of His Word by His Spirit. Don't put trust solely in my outlook nor lean solely to your own understanding. I pray that you'll agree with God's plan of salvation and His way to deliver you from every bondage known and unknown. I pray that you'll allow Him to bring your heart and the content of your heart into a greater light. I pray that you'll experience a greater liberty through Him. **Psalm 145:18** states that *"The Lord is nigh unto all them that call upon him, to all that call upon him in truth."*

It's been a while since the last interactive exercise. These are to keep your heart engaged. Pause now and take a moment to pray from your heart. It doesn't have to be a long prayer, just a sincere one from your heart. Let's do it together. Add to it as you are led to do so.

Heavenly Father, thank you for your grace that has preserved me for this moment.

I thank you for such an ordained time as this!

Guide my heart by your word and by your Spirit.

I yield my whole heart to you now.

Let your light shine in my heart to redeem it from all darkness.

Bring forth all the insights necessary to bring liberty in every area of my life. In Jesus' name. Amen.

I don't mind sharing my personal experiences because they're pieces to the big picture. Each experience is another piece of the puzzle that makes up the whole victory. They may be helpful in encouraging you although they're my testimonies. I hope that my transformation will help to push you forward to keep going until you receive your personal breakthrough. You'll ultimately have your own arsenal of stories to tell, because you'll only have one glorious breakthrough after another when you trust in the Father's leading.

I've shared a lot, even to the hurt of my own pride, knowing that it's worth it if it will help one person overcome one hurdle in their life. I pray that it will. The way to get over the hurdle is by conditioning your heart to know that it can. Whatever is in your heart weighs heavily in every decision that you make each day. This is why your heart must be examined, purged and kept upright. **Proverbs 4:23** says to *"Keep thy heart with all diligence; for out of it are the issues of life."* I recall that the U. S. Army had a slogan years ago that encouraged potential soldiers to "Be all that you can be." This is what the truth wants for you.

Unharness the power that will strengthen every part of your life that's lying dormant within. Yes, God gave you power to walk in this revelation. This power must be engaged, implemented and sometimes awakened to fulfill the things that God has ordered on your life. Use the power of prayer, faith, hope and endurance. God gave you power to unleash yourself from every yoke that minimizes triumph in you. It's your choice to do it. Use the power of choice to choose God's way.

I have five adorable grandchildren, four granddaughters and one grandson. One day I had a conversation with the youngest granddaughter, Roman. Roman would sometimes play a game with her sisters in which they would use their self-acclaimed super powers on one another. Now, I don't want anyone to get concerned or afraid. This wasn't some strange hokey pokey game. It was just a game they created after watching countless hours of movies in which they saw super heroes demonstrating these various super powers… the same type of hero shows we watched as kids.

So, being kids, they decided that they, too, would demonstrate a super power, and they all chose a super power for themselves. One would announce to the other one, "I use my superpower of "this" or "that," whatever it was, usually something like freezing, laughing, or jumping tall and so forth. Of course, they choose a super power that they felt gave them control, and they used it when it benefited them the most.

One day Roman said to me, wanting me to hold still, "Grandma, I use my superpower to freeze you so, you have to be frozen." Of course, I didn't obey the freezing command. So, she said it again, "Grandma, you're frozen," and again I refused to be still. She tried to explain to me that when the superpowers are being used on you, you have to do it. Of course, I refused to comply again. After a few times, Roman became a little irritated because I continued to move about unfrozen. Finally, she asked, "Grandma, I used my superpower to freeze you, why aren't you frozen?" I said, "because I'm using my superpower, too." So, she asked, "What's your superpower?" I said "choice and I don't choose to be frozen." The look on her face was priceless, in a good way. She looked so amazed. It was like a light came on inside of her. She didn't ask me to be frozen again.

The next day I was upstairs, but I heard Roman downstairs with her siblings and she was telling them that she had a new super power and it was the best one ever. The others wanted to know what was this new super power and asked, "Roman, what is it?" Romain said very courageously, "choice"! It was hilarious to me. I must admit that it made me smile, and it was a great liberating moment for Roman! She quickly learned that the power of "choice" outweighed all the other superpowers that her siblings could imagine. They tried, what if I use the power of this, they said. It doesn't matter because I can still use my choice, she'd say. What if I use the superpower of that, they'd say, and she'd say, it doesn't matter because I still have my choice. It wasn't long before they all agreed with Roman and said, "Yeah, choice is a great superpower." Wow! It was just a game they played, and most likely they'll move on to other games as they grow older, but I hope they'll never forget the power of choice. I hope that they'll always remember that. It's an incredible revelation for everyone to learn. Choice is an outstanding superpower to posse. Guess what? We all have it, and while it's awesome to have the power of choice, it's even better to use.

Exercising choice is an ancient thing. The act of choosing is nothing new. This is demonstrated in **Joshua 24:15** and in **2 Corinthians 10:5**. These biblical instructions were shared a long time ago; however, they have not changed. Today God still offers us the power to choose. Choice is a God-given right. You must choose to use it or not. It's up to you, it's up to me and it's up to each individual. You are presented with options every day. All anyone can ever do is present the case to you. They can present the benefits of the option, the disadvantages and/or consequences that are attached to the option, but the choice itself is always yours to make. These are Joshua's words in **Joshua 24:15**,

"And if it seem evil unto you to serve the LORD, choose you this day whom ye will; whether the gods which your fathers served that were on the other side of the flood, or the gods of the Amorites, in whose land ye dwell: but as for me and my house, we will serve the LORD."

Choices! What choices have you made that are now in deputizing positions within you? What choices have you given keys and authority to lock, enchain and/or liberate you? What things have you empowered to hold and bind you to a place not of God? Choices help and/or prevent you from reaching the divine will of God. You make choice after choice after choice. You are a choice maker, so choose what resides in your heart and what must go. While truth is the tool that reveals, you must still choose to implement necessary changes to progress into a better place. Learn to choose the thoughts that will abide in your mind and what thoughts are casted out of the mind. Yes, you are empowered to do this.

According to **2 Corinthians 10:5,** you should be *"Casting down imaginations, and every high thing that exalteth itself against the knowledge of God, and bringing into captivity every thought to the obedience of Christ."* You can only be mastered by a thing or a person you have chosen to serve. Am I saying that you can control the thoughts that enter your mind? No, I'm not. However, when a thought enters your mind that's not a thought you care to entertain because it doesn't align with the Word or will of God concerning you, you can cast that thought down IF you so choose to do so. That's power, and God has given that power to you to use.

Here are additional scriptures to let you know that you have this powerful gift of choice to equip you with even more assurance.

Romans 6:16 says, *"Know ye not, that to whom ye yield yourselves servants to obey, his servants ye are to whom ye obey; whether of sin unto death, or of obedience unto righteousness?".*

Yielding is the action that manifests the position of servitude. You choose to become its servant in this context when you yield to something. You're the one making the choice to yield to it whether it's to something good or bad.

According to the Blue Letter Bible Concordance, the word "yield"[1] in the previous scriptural reference comes from the Greek word "*paristem*. It means to bring into one's fellowship or intimacy. With whom are you choosing to be in fellowship with or agreeing to be intimate with? This is a probing question, I know, but God wants you to be conscious of the things you're choosing to yield to.

Furthermore, choice involves submission. Some form of submission is in operation when you make a choice. The same reference source stated that submission, as used in **Romans 10:3**, the next scriptural reference, comes from the Greek word "*hypotasso*". [2]Hypotasso means to subject one's self, to obey; to submit to one's control; to yield to one's admonition or advice; to obey, be subject; to submit to one's control. Simply put, submission and yielding to are both components of choice.

Romans 10:3 states, *"For they being ignorant of God's righteousness, and going about to establish their own righteousness, have not submitted themselves unto the righteousness of God."*

The heart must yield to and submit to the plan of God to receive God's intended results. God's promised results are attached to His plan. It's difficult to yield or submit to an unknown plan. God informed His people in **Jeremiah 29:11** that He had a plan. There were false plans being shared by man prior to His revealing it. These were false prophecies. They had good intentions; however, their plans were misleading because they weren't true. Finally, God shares His plan for the people through a prophet named Jeremiah. He stated, *"For I know the thoughts that I think toward you, saith the LORD, thoughts of peace, and not of evil, to give you an expected end."* So, you see the plan isn't unknown to the Planner, the plan is unknown to those who haven't yet had it revealed to them. You won't obtain the fullness of God's expected end without submitting wholeheartedly to God's plan, the plan He must make known to you.

The children of Israel were led to the Promised Land, which was the plan God had for them. However, to possess the land the children of Israel needed to meet the prerequisite of submitting to God's plan of possession of the land. They had to be willing to fight for it. They forfeited being able to take possession, although it was promised to them, because they were unable to follow God's instructions out of fear of someone else. A few of them were able to possess the land later on in life, but possession was still gained only by following God's directive plan. In other words, those few who possessed the land still had to fight for it, which was the original order of possession. They had to submit to the way of God that would give them the victory. They had to yield to God's divine will and to His divine way of obtaining what He desired for them. This is why you must give God full reign in your heart. **Luke 6:46** asks, *"And why call ye me, Lord, Lord, and do not the things which I say?"*. It's not enough to recognize that He is the Lord or even merely confess it by calling Him Lord: You must submit to His leading. You must submit to His Lordship. Submission is demonstrated through obedience. You must obey the Lord's will.

Matters of the heart are all of the things within you, all of the things that are buried deep, all of the things impacting your life directly or indirectly; these things place pressure and influence on your life's progress. You must surrender all these things to God, but you can't intentionally surrender to something that you don't know is there. You might do it accidently or by coincidence but not deliberately. When you have clear sight of it and surrender fully to God's plan concerning it – that's full submission.

God is the revealer of secrets, even the heart's secrets. Being the revealer of all secrets, why would He need you to tell Him anything? Why would someone who already sees all and knows all want you to tell Him about it? Why open your heart to tell Him what's already open to Him? These are legitimate questions. Let me share my thoughts on this. Telling God the matters of your heart isn't shared because He needs to know about them. It's for the purpose of Him revealing the root of the matter to you. The mass of what you need to know about your true self or a matter that you may be facing is hidden under layers of outward chaff. The truth isn't always as it appears. What you see on the surface is only partial. It's the reason it's called the tip of the iceberg. The tip of the iceberg only shows the tip, but there's much more ice underneath the surface that'd not seen. Only those who dare to dive deep enough will see the actual span of the iceberg. Only they will understand its full dimensions.

Likewise, the fruit you see on a tree didn't begin by being fruit. It started with something no longer seen on the surface at all, with a seed. A seed planted, buried and concealed, and if concealed, then unseen. This is the danger of looking

Outward only. Not everything outward is untrue; however, when the outward is your main focus and what you use to calculate, sum up and judge to be the truth, well, that can be deceiving. Look what's told to Samuel in the Book of **1 Samuel 16:7**. *"But the LORD said unto Samuel, Look not on His countenance, or on the height of His stature; because I have refused Him: for the LORD seeth not as man seeth; for man looketh on the outward appearance, but the LORD looketh on the heart."* Enough said. If the heart is what God has His eyes on, then it might be wise to focus on what matters most to God.

---

1. "yield," Blueletterbible.org, accessed August 26, 2020, https://www.blueletterbible.org/lang/lexicon/lexicon.cfm?Strongs=G3936&t=KJV
2. "hypotasso," Blueletterbible.org, accessed August 26, 2020, https://www.blueletterbible.org/lang/lexicon/lexicon.cfm?Strongs=G5293&t=KJV

You are invited...

It's never too late to give you this invitation. Throughout the book you've been given opportunities to engage. I hope you've been accepting the invitations to take steps towards your own redemption by way of truth. God constantly calls for your heart to draw near to Him. Every matter in your heart matters to Him. Be careful not to underestimate what you don't confront in your heart. Unconfronted matters are drivers, and sometimes, even victims and prisoners of whatever's ruling the heart. Whatever light there is in your heart or whatever darkness resides in your heart has power to persuade your heart. The content of your heart either drives your behavior or victimizes your heart, or a stronghold holds your heart captive to it. This goes on until you realize the truth or until you make new choices to remove the stronghold.

I repeat, truth breaks yokes. Truth is what makes the difference. God's people are people who should expect truth from

Him. They should desire it from Him and make it the reigning voice in their hearts.

Take the time to do the simple exercises that search your heart. Maybe you've been doing the ones that are sprinkled throughout this book. Perhaps you were doing this before you ever picked up this book. If so, that's great! I encourage you to continue and never stop. Make seeking God for the deliverance that's gained only through truth a perpetual seeking. This will keep you free inside. Consider this an official invitation if you honestly haven't yet been sold on the need to give God the matters of your heart. Please, make this book more than a read; make it a personal experience for you to be released from the things that weigh your heart down. Make it a witness that liberty from deception can be yours. You are invited to engage in life more abundantly. Remember, God looks at the heart; so, get your heart involved. Get to your "heart" work.

These simple activities, exercises, thought-provoking questions and borderline self-interrogations are to help reveal more of your heart to you. There are some subconscious thoughts and filters that need to be disturbed, unlocked and enlightened for you to see what you haven't been able to see or just haven't taken the time to act on. Why continue to weigh down your heart with these matters when release is available? Instead, get ready for an adventure!

Here's another chance to engage. It starts with a willing heart that's open to truth. You'll have an adventure of a lifetime if you're willing to go a little deeper. Ask yourself these questions and answer them truthfully from your heart.

- Are you willing to dive deeper into prayer to seek God for an honest assessment of your heart?
- Are you ready to explore closed-off areas within your heart?
- Are you ready to allow God to speak to the matters of your heart?

Taking time to pause and truthfully answer these and other simple questions like these will advance you further on your way to a magnificent new place. The heart is an adventurous place. There are thrilling things in there. There are unexpected heights, unrealized depths, many mysteries, unleashed joys and so much more.

You're going to be amazed! Your heart is capable of holding so much more than you'll ever know. It keeps taking in more and more until it's full; so, fill it with the love of God. Fill it with the passion of fulfilling God's will. Fill it with God's truth, and you'll see it flourish with freedom. Your heart will love you for it!

CRYOUT

AS WE COME TO A CLOSURE, WE COME TO NEW BEGINNINGS ...

This book is coming to a close, but before it does, I want to leave you with some guidance that will benefit you long after you read the book's last word. I know deliverance will come. In the meantime, CRYOUT!

CRYOUT! is an acronym or abbreviation. Use the C-R-Y-O-U-T-! abbreviation to help you remember to maintain your heart's liberty by truth. CRYOUT! every day. Be sincere. You'll experience some level of deliverance whenever you do these steps sincerely and from your heart. Truth, love, God's Word and the Holy Spirit will lead you all the way.

Mark 10:46-51 tells the story of a blind man named Bartimaeus. I'm paraphrasing here, but I give its actual recording below. Bartimaeus basically relied on others to meet his needs. He begged by the highway. One day he heard that Jesus was passing by, and he began to cry out, asking for mercy. He kept crying out and refused to stop until he received what he desired and needed to live a better life. Jesus didn't refuse his cry; instead, He met the beggar's true need, which was his sight. Neither will Jesus refuse your cry; He will supply your true need, whatever that may be, to make you whole.

Here's the actual account of what happened as it's written in **Mark 10:46-51**:

"And they came to Jericho: and as he went out of Jericho with His disciples and a great number of people, blind Bartimaeus, the son of Timaeus, sat by the highway side begging.

And when he heard that it was Jesus of Nazareth, he began to cry out, and say, Jesus, thou Son of David, have mercy on me.

And many charged him that he should hold peace: but he cried the more a great deal, Thou Son of David, have mercy on me.

And Jesus stood still, and commanded him to be called. And they call the blind man, saying unto him, Be of good comfort, rise; he calleth thee.

And he, casting away his garment, rose, and came to Jesus.

And Jesus answered and said unto him, What wilt thou that I should do unto thee?

The blind man said unto Him, Lord, that I might receive my sight.

And Jesus said unto him, Go thy way; thy faith hath made thee whole.

And immediately he received his sight, and followed Jesus in the way."

CRYOUT! isn't a routine. It's a process that will build your relationship with God. Use it for the purpose of drawing closer to the One who will not only meet your outward need but will also address the root cause of the need. So, CRYOUT! with your whole heart. **Colossians 3:23** states, *"And whatsoever ye do, do it heartily, as unto the Lord, and not unto men."* Do it heartily. God wants your whole heart because He wants you to live life whole-heartedly and complete in him.

"Confess"

Here's where you begin with the CRYOUT! process. The first letter, "**C**," is to remind you to "Confess. This is the first step to becoming better at anything. Even ten-step programs will advise you that you must first admit that you have a problem before you can begin to resolve it. You must acknowledge the truth, the truth of who you are, where you are and where you're headed.

Confession calls for yet another self-assessment. You must take inventory and personal ownership of what you find.

This book has been preparing you to be comfortable asking yourself simple locating questions. In doing so, you must always be honest with your responses. The self-probing questions you ask yourself don't have to be deep, two-part or five-part questions, just simple ones that will help you to identify where you are as you begin your journey.

So, begin with simple ones like the ones below. Then add more as you begin to unfold your heart. The search is on and it starts here.

- Who are you?
- Where are you?
- Where are you headed?

Why is this necessary? Well, if your goal is to embark to a new place, then, most likely you would need a map. You're off to a good start if you're looking at a map of where you wanted to go and are ready to make the commitment to get there. The first thing you would need to do is locate your present spot. Find your present location on the map of where you're trying to go. Then, locate where you're headed and follow the directions that will to get you there. The terrain may change as you move forward. The road will be smooth at times and bumpy at other times, but stay the course and you'll get there.

Denial of where you are will not help you get where you're trying to go. Refusing to admit truth, whatever that truth may be, will not help you arrive at your new place of breakthrough. This truth may be painful to face. It may cause disturbance in your heart as it's realized, uncovered or confronted, but let the light of truth in. It's the only way that you'll become free from the bondage that accompanies not facing the truth. Remember, take sobering moments. Take time away from the noise. You need time away from the crowd and the persuasive voices that will not allow you to hear those undisturbed truths that are hindering you from being joyfully free.

Once you've allowed yourself to see what these real matters of your heart are, then confess them to God. Confess to Him where you are according to your own calculations: who you are and where you're headed. Now, you're open to honesty. Now, you're open to truth. Now, be open to hear His voice. Now, you're open to receiving the change that will manifest in your heart and ultimately in your life as a result of taking this step of confession.

Closets! Yes, closets; this is what's referred to as the place where these confessions are made, the place of separation where you go talk with God away from everything and everyone else. God's Word calls this place your closet. It's the place where you go to pray. In this place and within this prayer, confessions are definitely a part of the conversation that you should have with God. This is a real place of crying out where God has committed to see you. Furthermore, He commits to respond to you.

Matthew 6:6 states, *"But thou, when thou prayest, enter into thy closet, and when thou hast shut thy door, pray to thy Father which is in secret; and thy Father which seeth in secret shall reward thee openly."*

Hebrews 10:22 states, *"Let us draw near with a true heart in full assurance of faith, having our hearts sprinkled from an evil conscience, and our bodies washed with pure water."* There's a space known as "personal" space when you're speaking with people. It isn't physically marked, but it's a boundary that most people are aware of and respect. Violating that space can be viewed as an "in your face" experience. This is why most people stay at a comfortable distance when speaking to someone in person.

However, it's quite the contrary when speaking with God. He loves an "in your face" conversation. He loves the up-closeness when you draw near to Him with a true heart. He loves the closeness and tells us to draw near with a true heart. He wants us to come to Him, but He wants us to come pure and clean. David, the psalmist, wrote in **Psalms 24:3-6**, *"Who shall ascend unto the hill of the Lord? or who shall stand in his holy place? He that hath clean hands, and a pure heart; who hath not lifted up his soul unto vanity, nor sworn deceitfully."*

Understand this: The confession is for you. God is All Knowing. This process is for your benefit, so make your confession a good confession. Start with what you honestly know to be the truth about you, the things you're facing, the help you feel you need, your willingness to hear from Him. Start with an honest assessment of your heart. He will meet you where you are. Engage your heart as you lift up these confessions, and He will begin a work of liberation.

Here's an example of a prayer of confession to get you started. This doesn't have to be your actual prayer; it's a sample prayer in case you need help. The sample prayer is general; feel free to be detailed in your personal prayer of confession and open with your heart as you pray.

Sample prayer of confession

Lord, I confess that I have need of you that's beyond my understanding at this time.

I'm not leaning to my own understanding. I'm trusting in your guidance.

There are things inside of my heart that I've not allowed you to touch because of the pain I'm afraid the disturbance will cause.

I acknowledge that you are love, and you are wise, and you are more than capable of dealing with every part of my being, whether hidden or revealed.

Therefore, I confess these things and ask that you will reveal my whole heart to me and the hearts of all those directly or indirectly connected to me so that deliverance may come.

Draw all hearts to you and lead all hearts to victory. In Jesus' name. Amen.

The prayer of salvation is another confession prayer that's important. If you have not prayed a prayer confessing Jesus as Lord and you would like to, then you can use this sample prayer of confession for salvation below.

Sample prayer of confession for salvation

Lord, I pray the prayer of confession for salvation according to **Romans 10:9-10** *that states, "That if thou shalt confess with* *thou mouth the Lord Jesus, and shalt believe in thine heart that God hath raised him from the dead, thou shalt be saved. For with the heart man believeth unto righteousness; and with the mouth confession is made unto salvation."*

I make this confession now as I believe with my heart. In Jesus' name. Amen.

"Repent"

Oh, the "**R**" word. The word that humbles us all and makes us all look guilty of having done something wrong. The truth is that we're all guilty of having done something wrong. So, please my friend, with everything that's within you, don't shun repentance. This is a crucial step in maintaining an authentic relationship with God, our Heavenly Father. Embrace repentance as the blessing that it is. A blessing is exactly what repentance is for those who want to be upright before God. Repentance is the act of acknowledging our sins, the wrongs we have performed in actions, thoughts or deeds and are guilty of. Repentance gets us past the starting line of confessing the sin.

Sin. This is another one of those "things" that's agreed upon as it relates to its existence, but sin isn't so easily owned or claimed. There are no big sins or little sins, it's all just sin. Any sin refers to the things or actions performed in violation of God's established law. Everyone has fallen short of meeting them all. Thankfully, grace is there to help when this occurs. Grace isn't presented as an ongoing free pass to continue to sin, it's not permission to practice a life of sin. Regardless of grace, however, repentance of sin is still required. We are expected to repent for wrongdoings even with grace.

Repentance is the heart's way of saying "I'm sorry" to God. Repentance admits from the heart those wandering actions that strayed off of the path of uprightness. It admits to missing the mark, making the error and owning up to the mistake. The sin performed is performed against God. David taught this lesson as he repented in **Psalm 51:4**. He admitted the following in this particular text, *"Against thee, thee only have I sinned, and done this evil in thy sight: that thou mightest be justified when thou speakest, and be clear when thou judgest."*

Where there is sin, there is an offence against God. Where there is sin, there is a need for grace, because sin carries with it an eternal penalty of death and separation from God. These scriptural references will help shed additional light on the undeniable need to repent and the part grace plays in the matter.

Acts 3:19a: *"Repent ye therefore, and be converted, that your sins may be blotted out."* Sin doesn't fade away; it must be repented of. Failure to repent leaves the root of sin intact, and it won't be long before the fruit of the sin manifests.

Romans 6:23: *"For the wages of sin is death; but the gift of God is eternal life through Jesus Christ our Lord."* The penalty is still enforceable if the repentance isn't made. You don't get to have both a life of unrepented sin and the gift of life. The gift is in receiving Christ, which calls for repentance.

Romans 5:20 speaks to the blessing of grace, stating, *"Moreover the law entered, that the offence might abound. But where sin abounded, grace did much more abound."* While grace abounds, it doesn't abound that sin might continue. Grace is a gift that gives you the space and the chance to repent for breaking God's divine law.

Romans 6:1-2 explains the relationship between sin and grace this way, *"What shall we say then? Shall we continue in sin, that grace may abound? God forbid. How shall we, that are dead to sin, live any longer therein?"*. Grace is not a ticket granting a pass to continue doing the things that are contrary to God's will.

Grace offers the opportunity to repent. It allows those who have the desire to realign themselves from a wandered path to approach the throne of God by confessing and repenting. Grace is the opportunity for those who are godly sorrowful in their heart for the wrong they committed against God to turn from these wrongs.

Repentance is more than admitting a wrongful act against God's way. The Book of 2 Corinthians 7:10a speaks in part to godly sorrow as being the source that works repentance. It states *"For godly sorrow worketh repentance to salvation not to be repented of."*. Repentance is birthed from a godly sorrow, which means that you don't have a desire to repeat the action because it brings you sorrow for offending God. True repentance comes from a heart that's been pricked to do better, a heart to turn away from the sin act and a heart to live life forward in the restored status that was granted through repentance.

God is waiting to hear your prayer of repentance. Here's a sample prayer you can use to get started. These prayer samples aren't shared to insinuate that this is the format that you must follow; they're models that provide examples of how you might start your conversation around repentance with God. Feel free to use the model prayer or pray as you're led by your heart's sincerity. The main thing is that you pray a prayer of repentance each day to keep your heart free from things that are in opposition to God's will.

Sample prayer of repentance

Father in heaven, hallowed be thy name.

I humbly repent for every deed made within my body, thought within my mind, held within my heart and soul that did not line up with your will for my life.

I ask for forgiveness for taking matters into my own hands and not seeking you for guidance.

Cause me to develop a habit of seeking you first so that you can direct my path.

Renew me as I yield my heart for your cleansing.

I repent for all my sins and renounce all forms of rebelling against your word and your will consciously or subconsciously.

I turn away from the things that you reveal are in my heart but are not pleasing to you. In Jesus' name. Amen.

"Yield"

The whole point of the CRYOUT process is to keep seeking God so He can reveal your heart. **Luke 11:9** *says, "And I say unto you, Ask, and it shall be given you; seek, and ye shall find; knock, and it shall be opened unto you."* God is faithful to answer and reveal.

Seeing that your heart is great at playing the game of "*Hide and Seek*", there are things hidden within it that will require an all-seeing eye to point it out. You must be open and your heart yielded to God and to truth to receive the fullness of life and experience His liberty.

This is why the letter "**Y**" in the CRYOUT acronym is to remind you to "yield." This part is going to be short and quick. There are unyielded matters in your heart. They're unyielded because they're unrevealed, and if unrevealed and unyielded, then they're definitely unsubmitted.

You have to know the truth to be totally submitted to truth. What you choose to yield to, you choose to submit to as a servant. It's important to get to the truth so you'll not be submitted to the deceptions of half-truths and plain old lies.

Romans 10:3 states, *"For they being ignorant of God's righteousness, and going about to establish their own righteousness, have not submitted themselves unto the righteousness of God."*

Paul speaks of a people who didn't know God's righteousness, so they established their own righteousness; in doing so, though they were submitted to their truth, it wasn't the real truth at all. **Romans 3:4a** says in part, *"let God be true, but every man a liar."* Remember, the goal of yielding is to trust the leading of God by His Spirit. I know this sounds far-fetched, but it isn't.

God wants to commune with you by His Spirit. Seek Him first, and He will use whomever or whatever He deems to be necessary to lead you by truth. He will use a dream, a vision, the scriptures, an obedient servant submitted unto Him or no one. Yes, he can bring you into His will miraculously with no man's help. Deliverance is of Him. He is able alone. This is why seeking Him is vital and yielding to Him even more than vital; it's an absolute must.

Jesus teaches in **John 14:26** that the Father sent a gift called the Holy Ghost who is a Comforter, sent to help those who would receive Him. Jesus said, *"But the Comforter, which is the Holy Ghost, whom the Father will send in my name, he shall teach you all things, and bring all things to your remembrance,* *whatsoever I have said unto you."* The Holy Ghost will remind you of truth.

Yield your whole heart to His leading. He will not go contrary to the true way, God's Word. They're one in agreement, one and the same, inseparable. You'll be freed of whatever strongholds, known or unknown, exist in your life due to untruths. Their grip will be broken the more you yield to truth. Yes, **John 8:32** again, *"And ye shall know the truth, and the truth shall make you free."* Here's a sample prayer for yielding to get you started now.

Sample prayer for yielding

Lord, I yield my whole heart to you.

As you tug on my heart, leading me away from deception by your word and your Spirit, help me not to draw back.

I yield my heart to embrace the truth revealed as I seek you in prayer, your Word, and by your Spirit.

Grant unto me discernment to know your voice. Teach me to yield to your ways and to resist wrongful influences.

I'm your yielded vessel. I submit to your leading. In Jesus' name. Amen.

"Obey"

Proverbs 4:7 says, *"Wisdom is the principal thing; therefore get wisdom: and with all thy getting get understanding."* You can make better choices about whether to accept or reject something when you understand its significance. Doing what you're asked without your heart's engagement is compliance. It takes a willing heart to totally surrender in obedience. The letter "**O**" in the CRYOUT! acronym is for "Obedience. Don't stop at compliance for the sake of complying. Engage your heart in obeying the truth.

Obedience is what God wants from you. You will not obtain or benefit from reconciliation, deliverance or breakthroughs without obedience to His Word. You will not be able to maintain your victory if you don't continue to obey the truth. You must not only receive truth, you must also obey truth. **Galatians 5:7** reads, *"Ye did run well; who did hinder you that ye* *should not obey the truth?"*. Obedience to the directions of the revealed truth never stops; it has no end date.

Take note here that hindrance comes after disobedience to truth. Refusing the truth interferes with the progress. It interrupts the advancements gained from obeying the truth. Remember, the truth has the power to make you free, but if you disobey it, you forfeit the liberty it brings.

Here's a prayer sample that will help keep your heart surrendered to obedience to truth, God's truth according to His Word. Modify this prayer as needed to align your heart with God's obedience. I understand that this book will not be received by all, not even by all who choose to read it, because not everyone wants to obey the truth to achieve their true victory, but that's where the victory lies, and that's the only way you'll keep the victory once it's obtained.

Prayer example for obedience

Father God, the only one who knows all and sees all, I come before you with a heart that's ready to obey your leading.

I understand in choosing to obey you, it will eventually require me to make sacrifices, as I may not always be able to have my way in choosing to obey yours… and I'm ok with that.

Help me to obey you because you are God, and that alone is a good enough reason to do it.

Give me the strength to do this daily. In Jesus' name. Amen.

"Uncover"

We're now at the letter "**U**" in the CRYOUT! Acronym. This is to remind you to "Uncover." Uncovering causes you to face your realities. Don't be afraid to take off the mask. Getting to the core of matters may call for uncovering many layers. This can be a deterrent to some, but don't put limits on the possibilities of your outcome.

Don't worry about being naked and vulnerable before truth. This is part of the process of you becoming stronger and more refined as the filters are removed. Truth will replace false securities and become a cover for you. Just as He did for Adam and Eve in the garden, God Himself will provide you a covering.

Psalm 91:4 says, *"He shall cover thee with His feathers, and under His wings shalt thou trust: His truth shall by thy shield and buckler."* He will not leave you naked.

It's vital that matters buried deeply within are exposed so they can be sorted out. The purpose of uncovering your heart before God in an effort to become free will prove beneficial for you and those directly or indirectly connected to you.

As with the other steps, continue to pray that you stay in this place of removing layers. Take daily steps to prevent the rebuild up of layers that can clog the heart with deception. Build up in the heart can cause a heart attack, maybe not a physical heart attack, but in this case an attack of bondage. The goal is to become free and stay free.

Here is a prayer sample for uncovering the heart. This is only to get you started. Keep going until you know that you have removed every barrier present to block the entering in of the truth, the whole truth and nothing but the truth, so help you God.

Prayer for uncovering the heart

Dear Lord, only you can see the number of layers that are covering my heart.

Make my heart bare before you. Strip away every filter preventing truth from reaching the core of my heart.

Uncover and reveal those things that are within me and need to be revealed to land me in a better place.

I know it's only after I face the hidden things that are influencing my heart will I able to move forward with clarity and understanding.

So, uncover my faith and let it come forth in all I do.

Uncover my joy so it can break forth in my song.

Uncover the strength that's there suppressed under tiers of veils, hiding beneath a plethora of pretenses, all wearing the mask of smiles and acceptable clichés.

Help me get to the bottom of "it" so that its matters will be settled for good.

Father cover me with your covering. In Jesus' name. Amen.

"Triumph"

You are more than a conqueror! That's not an opinion, it's God's truth. Paul relays this message in **Romans 8:37** but not before he described all of the oppositions that could arise. It shows that the fights will come, but victory will always belong to those who remain in truth. Well, actually, it states, *"Nay, in all these things we are more than conquerors through him that loved us."* The "him" in the scriptural reference here is referring to Christ. Christ is truth. He is *"the way, the truth and the life"* according to **John 14:6a.**

The overcoming victory is yours when you abide in and operate in love despite the circumstances you face. Your hardships don't have to destroy you. You can triumph every time with truth. The "**T**" in CRYOUT! is for "Triumph, triumph by trusting in God for this process.

Rid yourself of everything that hinders you from being your true self. Don't play the games. Let the "you" the Creator created live without apology. Live life more abundantly for Him who has broken every chain of the enemy off of you. Live triumphantly for Him who has taken you through every challenge and made you the champion over chaos.

No more pressed down, settled for, half-hearted living but a life that has been liberated from within, from the heart. Wow! This is such a reality. God wants this for you. It doesn't matter what's going on in the world, who is "ruling" or who is appearing to reign over it.

Psalms 24:1 says, *"The earth is the Lord's, and the fullness thereof; the world, and they that dwell therein."* God is still God, and He is still in control.

Proverbs 16:7 states, *"When a man's ways please the Lord, he maketh even his enemies to be at peace with him."* No matter what the matters are that you face, trusting in God to get you through them is the only way you'll win this fight called life.

Pray, pray, always pray. Prayer is a way of God. It's how you stay connected to Him. I know, I've said it once. I've said it twice. I keep saying it because it's true. It's your key to overcoming the many obstacles that can arise. Prayer will get you through them all.

Here is a sample prayer for seeking God for the victory. You can be triumphant but not without God, not without truth and not without letting go and letting God. You must let go of doing it your way and let God lead you to your victory. The victory belongs to Him, but He will give it to you when you're under His leading. Everything will work out for your good when you do.

Sample prayer for triumph

Master! King of Kings and Lord of Lords! God Almighty, I come to you thanking you for the victory.

I don't have to wait until the battle is over to rejoice, because I'm turning the battle over to you and you never lose.

Thank you for causing me to triumph by your power.

I stand in the victory that you have granted through my submission to your will.

Teach me to maintain the victory that I received by the blood of Jesus, the Lamb of God that was slain and took away my sins, my shortcomings and defeat.

I take hold of the gift of Christ. By His power I overcome all the powers of darkness, strongholds, barriers, deceptions and anything that comes to steal or rob me of the victorious life that's mine through Him, my victorious champion.

I receive this victory now. In Jesus' name. Amen. Hallelujah!

"Be excited about it"

What's the "point" after doing all of this? It's an exclamation point! Get it? Yes, even the exclamation point has a meaning in the CRYOUT! acronym. This mark (!) is a mark used to add emotional intensity. It's the grammatical symbol that represents loudness, such as a scream, an outcry or a shout! It denotes excitement!

God wants you to be excited about bringing the matters of your heart before Him. He wants you to be happy, to be glad and not bear a heavy heart. Don't let the warfare or the cares of this world bring you down. Instead, have the joy of knowing you can bring everything to Him in prayer. There is mercy and grace available for you.

Hebrews 4:16 says, *"Let us therefore come boldly to the throne of grace, that we may obtain mercy, and find grace to help in time of need."* This is great news!

You can enter into this process knowing that there is a throne of grace. Grace will walk you through the process. Grace will lead you every step of the way. Grace will cover you in your confession, repentance, yielding, the stripping of disobedience, and the uncovering of layers to the triumph! What an exciting journey!

Sample prayer, yes even for this (!):

Oh, Mighty God of Deliverance! I give you praise!

Thank you for all of your goodness! Your love for me is more than I'm able to comprehend!

Thank you for setting me free indeed and for granting life more abundantly!

I give you the glory for the changes brought about in my life that are fostered by the changes brought abought in my heart!

I love you Lord, my God, with my whole heart! In Jesus' name. Amen!

In conclusion...

Well, my friend, I'm close to the conclusion of my assignment. I've almost released everything that I was led by the Holy Spirit to release. I know that lives will be changed in following these processes. I know that my life was changed by them. I also know in my heart that this book needed to be finished so that it can get into the hands of those who are seeking to be free from the burdens of their heart.

My testimony, God's grace; my deliverance, God's doing! The matters of your heart sincerely matter to God. He knows your heart, He knows what it's capable of, He knows its burdens, and He knows how to make it free. He does it in love, He does it in truth, and He does it His way, but He doesn't fail! Greatness awaits you through His plan. It's yours if you dare accept His gracious offer.

This is the end of the outpouring I was given to share for this assignment, but it's nowhere near the end of all that God has yet to say about truth, prayer, deliverance, breakthroughs or the heart. I encourage you to continue to seek the Lord for all of your answers, because He is the answer to all of life's problems.

Do me a favor: share your story of deliverance and spread the wonderful news of how it's God's desire that everyone would turn their hearts and the matters of their hearts to Him that He might make them free, indeed!

This is my story. He's still doing it for me. I know He will do it for you, too!

Acts 10:34 says, *"Then Peter opened his mouth, and said, Of a truth I perceive that God is no respecter of persons."*

My prayer for you

May the peace of God be with you – always!

May the lovingkindness of God draw you into the fullness of His redemption.

May God continuously and forever bless you and cause your heart to sing!

In Jesus' Mighty name I pray – Amen and Amen!

About the Author

Bridget Dixon is a servant leader. She pastors two churches; *The Sword of the Lord Church Intl.* in LaGrange GA; and *Ambassador for Christ Discipleship and Outreach Church, Intl.* in College Park, GA.

Of the latter, she established a 501(C)3 non-profit organization that supports various communities in Georgia by supplying monthly discipleship, bible studies and community events.

She's an active advocate for the elderly, hungry and homeless and, leads the "*Feed the Hungry, Clothe the Naked*" initiative which solicits for and, provides food and clothing to those in need.

Bridget supports the eradication of inequality and co-organized "*March for Equality*"; a one-mile nonviolent community protest against inequality and injustice.

She served on several mission trips as a witness of her Christian faith, and in sharing the love of Christ with others. Her mission travels included Las Vegas, Mexico, Jamaica, Israel and two trips to Haiti.

Bridget is married to Morris Dixon of 36 years, the mother to Morris L. Dixon and Christina Shipmon and, "Grandma" to Sarah, Qar'Mah, Roman and Kingston; and Qyryanna (grandma in heart).